# Juicy AF*

# Juicy AF*

## Stop the Drinking Spiral, Create Your Future

### KAY ALLISON

JUICY AF*

*Stop the Drinking Spiral, Create Your Future*

ISBN   HARDCOVER: 978-1-5445-3686-6
       PAPERBACK: 978-1-5445-3687-3
       EBOOK: 978-1-5445-3688-0

*To the beautiful, vibrant sisters who
show me how to be joyfully alcohol-free.*

*And to my Darling Husband, without whom
my AF life would be much less juicy.*

# CONTENTS

# INTRODUCTION

I'M FIVE EIGHT and I have strikingly blue eyes. I drank a lot and my life was stalled out. Like my height and eye color, I thought my drinking habits and stalled life were simply uncorrelated facts: They both just WERE and had nothing to do with each other.

I also thought everyone drank the way I drank. My girlfriends (or at least most of them) did. The guys I dated, too. Same for my advertising colleagues. It honestly never occurred to me that anyone lived any other way.

But what I eventually learned—after far too much unnecessary confusion, pain, and drama—was the way I drank and my stuck life were indeed correlated. Not only that, but the relationship was CAUSAL. Drinking was at the root of my problems.

I was absolutely shocked, though in retrospect I probably shouldn't have been.

## Where It All Started

In high school, I was a total good girl during the week. I got straight As and was in all honors classes. Come the weekends, though— watch out. Bad girl! Keggers were my jam.

I was only a freshman the first time I drank. A junior asked me to go to a party with him and as soon as we walked in, someone handed me a red cup full of beer. I gleefully accepted it, chugged it down, and went looking for some more.

Coming back from the keg—with a full cup, of course—I noticed a cute guy playing guitar in the living room. The more I drank, the cuter he looked. Before long, I had a great buzz and was literally rolling around on the floor with Guitar Guy. Damn, was he a good kisser.

As you might imagine, Mr. Junior was not pleased. He still drove me home but left me at my door with a snide comment. "SOMEBODY had a little too much to drink tonight."

But his disappointment in me was no match for my excitement. I couldn't wait for the next party, the next Guitar Guy, or that next red cup full of beer. And I didn't need to worry—there would be plenty more of those to come, along with plenty more people I'd hurt and disappoint.

I was raised in a serious, studious, careful home where I felt like a misfit, and drinking was a vibrant counterpoint to that. It was brighter, more fun, and more stimulating than the environment I grew up in. It meant sociability and interaction. Like me, it was outgoing and colorful and a little bit reckless. It seemed to fit me like a glove.

So, for the rest of high school, I continued down the same path: model student Monday through Friday, keg parties all weekend. In college, I started dating a much older guy and those keggers morphed into more sophisticated affairs with better alcohol choices. He took me to cocktail parties (very glam!) and formal events (even more glam!). He could buy liquor easily (a bonus—I was still underage). We drank heavily together, and as my love affair with him deepened, so did my love for drinking.

After college, I started working as an account executive at a prestigious global ad agency. I quickly rose up the ranks using a combo of brains, a killer work ethic, and steely determination. By the time

I was twenty-eight, I was the company's youngest vice president. I was also drinking as much as ever.

At some point—it's hard to tell exactly when the shift happened—I developed two troubling patterns. The first was that once I had a single sip of wine or beer or whatever, it was like my off switch completely disappeared. I'd start to feel tipsy and all I wanted was more. And more. And MORE.

My brake stopped working and a crazed lead foot took over the gas pedal. Even if my intention was not to drink very much, I had no control over the amount I actually drank (not EVERY time, mind you, but MOST of the time, which was totally confusing). After I got started, I couldn't always guarantee I would stop at one or two. What I've since come to understand is that kind of craving and lack of control meant my relationship with alcohol was Trouble with a capital T.

*Where's the waiter, where's the waiter, can I get to the bar, order a quick vodka, slam it, and get back to the table without anyone noticing?*

I'd go out thinking I'd only get pleasantly buzzed and then cross that line so fast I couldn't even wave at it. I went from one sip to shit-faced with blazing speed. And then I'd just keep going until I "went to bed" (which was probably closer to passing out rather than fueled by any rational decision-making process).

In the morning, I'd wake up feeling wretched and immediately start trying to reconstruct what I did the night before: who I pissed off, who I drunk dialed, and what I drunk bought. I remember wondering *was that a blackout?* I could recall moments and parts of the night before, but my memory was totally blurry after a certain point. My hungover emotions—which consisted mainly of the lovely triumvirate of remorse, depression, and shame—were intense and all over the place.

Which leads me to the second troubling pattern: I'd always swear to myself *never again.* I'd resolve that this was the last time I'd ever do this to myself. And then I would always "change my mind."

What this meant was I never knew when or if I was going to start drinking again, and once I started, when or if I was going to stop. I could have been going to meet the President of the United States and if someone handed me a drink prior to that encounter, I would have no control over whether or not I'd drink it or how long I'd keep on drinking if I started. This was a terrifying realization.

Hungover, I'd waste most of the day trying just to get back to normal. I'd attempt to be productive and brilliant at work despite being physically and mentally wrecked. I'd go to the gym, hoping to sweat all the alcohol out of my system. I'd meditate in an effort to quash my inner harangue. All nice tries, but no dice.

By the end of the day, I'd still feel so shitty and have so much internal stress and agitation stirred up inside of me that a sip of white wine always started to sound like the perfect antidote. I'd tell myself, "Last night wasn't THAT bad. Maybe I'll have just one to take the edge off."

And then the whole cycle would start over. Once I started, I couldn't stop. Once I stopped, I always started again. Rinse and repeat. The dreaded spiral, in full effect.

Remember in *Sleeping Beauty* where she was cursed to prick her finger on the spindle of a spinning wheel and die? Well, alcohol was my spinning wheel. I was inexorably drawn to touch its spindle every time. And for a while there, it really seemed like it was going to be the death of me—or at least any person I WANTED to be.

Because after becoming so successful so quickly in advertising, I just couldn't seem to make the next move. I didn't understand why I wasn't going any further, or why I often felt so much less creative. My career path was stalled, and my income was, too. It never occurred to me that my drinking might have had something to do with any of that.

The quality of men I attracted drastically declined, too—I was now being pursued by the kind of guys who were accused of insider trading and downing a gallon of martinis at lunch. Take my daughter's best friend's uncle, who I met at her bat mitzvah, for example (I know that sounds like the beginning of a terrible joke, but no such luck). We were on a date with a bunch of people at a fancy steakhouse, and he said something rude to me—honestly, I couldn't even remember immediately afterward exactly what that was—so I stormed off. I have no idea how I got home. He then proceeded to call me every ten minutes, all night long, and I proceeded to refuse to pick up any of those calls. My drinking (plus his drinking) couldn't have possibly contributed to that kind of chaos, right?

Not to mention my standards in terms of what was acceptable behavior also went down the tubes. Drunk me did things I would never, ever do sober. I drove drunk. I went home with random guys. I had an affair with a client. None of it aligned with my real morals and values.

At my lowest point, my idea of a good time was eating four desserts, throwing them up, and then sleeping with somebody else's husband. I was a total riot, if you consider bulimia and having sex with married men a good time. Yet I STILL didn't put two and two together. I mean, I was a Senior Vice President at a global ad agency. My kids lived with me. I had friends and did yoga. It all LOOKED good. But it really wasn't.

Through it all, I never in a million years thought drinking could harm me physically, or even lead to death. That was for old dudes who lived under bridges and got cirrhosis of the liver, not nice, smart, well-educated women like me. What I've since learned— through painful experience watching people I've known drop like flies—is if there are "Fifty Ways to Leave Your Lover," there must be "One Thousand Ways to Die from Drinking."

And if the booze doesn't kill you? Well, there's always a tree to end up wrapped around and maimed by, a pedestrian to run over, or a prison cell waiting with your name on it. All of which happened to friends of mine who had alcohol problems but didn't quit or relapsed because they forgot to stay vigilant.

## Where Are You Starting From?

Does any of this sound familiar? Even just parts of it? Little smidgens here and there?

Your circumstances might be different, but if the way I felt and the way I drank rings any bells, I want you to know that I see you. I feel you. I've BEEN you. If you relate to how my body metabolizes alcohol, if you feel uncomfortable in your own skin, if you can't resist the glass of wine to take the edge off at the end of the day, I get it.

My guess is you're here because you have a sneaking suspicion that drinking isn't working that well for you, or at least not anymore. That sometimes you think you might want to stop drinking, or at least so much. That you feel like shit when you wake up hungover two or three times a week, say "never again," and then never again becomes yet again by five o'clock that same night. And maybe that used to happen once a month, but now it's happening a couple of times a week.

Been there.

Covid probably only accelerated the situation, and now you find yourself at least a little bit sober curious. Watching people like Adele, Chrissy Teigen, and Jennifer Garner hop on the wagon and start living their best lives without drinking makes you think, *hey, maybe I could do that, too.* Maybe you've even started inching your way toward changing your drinking habits—read one of the popular quit-lit books, tried doing Dry January, stalked the Stop Drinking subreddit, or ordered mocktails when you were out (and found it vaguely or maybe even not-so-vaguely unsatisfying)—but don't quite have the motivation to go all in just yet.

Been there, too.

I also wonder if you might be feeling as lost, alone, and isolated as I used to. Your career might feel a bit flat. You're starting to worry a bit about your health. Or your looks (drinkers' lines, anyone?). I bet you've tried all sorts of things—meditation, yoga, therapy, everything, anything—to feel better, but none of it had the kind of life-changing impact you were hoping it would. You know something isn't right in your life, but you're just not sure exactly what that is.

Well now, I've DEFINITELY been there.

If all this is ringing true, you're in absolutely the right place. This book is for anyone who is:

- Sober curious
- Wanting to "drink less"
- Sick of being hungover
- Tired of the drinking-remorse-drinking spiral
- Feeling mystified that they can solve so many other issues in their life but not control their drinking
- Trying to figure out why their career isn't going the way they want
- Feeling lost and hopeless and unsure of what to try next
- Unable to imagine life being fun without drinking

I am honored to know you. I'm delighted (and relieved) you're here. Welcome! I invite you to walk through the rest of this process together with me.

## How It Was Going

I had been drinking for more than half of my existence by the time I turned thirty-nine. I knew my life wasn't what I wanted or expected it to be, and I knew I was sick of feeling shitty—both mentally and physically—so much of the time. What I still hadn't figured out, though, was how inextricably connected those two things were. I was like Hansel and Gretel following that little bread crumb trail.

After nearly a decade of disappointing myself in a myriad of ways, I was driving to work one morning when I was struck with a terribly sobering thought: *I've already been hungover four days this week. If I live forty more years like this, that means I'll be hungover for at least twenty of them.* It felt like a giant revelation, though not quite revelatory enough to get me to quit drinking just yet.

It did, however, motivate me to write a strategic plan of things I wanted to accomplish before I turned forty. (Once a strategic planner, always a strategic planner!) One of the bullet points on it was to drink less. Among my proposed methods were: drink more juice, alternate water with wine, only drink on certain nights of the week, and only have a certain number of drinks on nights I was drinking. As a last-ditch option, I added a final possibility: go to one of "those" meetings. It was there only in case everything else failed (and maybe not even then).

Spoiler alert: none of my proposed ways of drinking less worked. I still had no off switch, no brake, and a lead foot on the gas pedal most of the time. Once I started with one drink, I'd inevitably blow off all my self-imposed rules. I'd "change my mind," or conveniently forget they existed in the first place. And I'd always start drinking again despite my best intentions.

For my fortieth birthday, I threw myself this really grandiose party that I couldn't begin to afford (because my main goal in life at the time was impressing other people). I had it catered. There were servers. Friends from all over the country flew in to celebrate with me.

I had enough foresight to realize *I want to enjoy this over-the-top expensive party as much as possible, so I'm going to try to stay present and only drink Diet Coke all night.* Which, of course, was a great plan until an impossibly handsome waiter with a sparkling silver tray came by and asked me one too many times if I wanted a glass of champagne. Have I mentioned how much I used to adore champagne? I thought, *I'll just have one.*

That first glass was gone before the waiter was. So I took another one. And then another. And who knows how many more. The next thing I (sort of) remember was my kids, who were ten and sixteen at the time, putting me to bed.

When I woke up the next morning, I was full of my usual remorse, depression, and shame. No surprise there. What DID surprise me, though, was that those familiar emotions had brought a new friend along with them this time: clarity.

I finally made the connection. Drinking was indeed causing problems in my life. Maybe it was even the cause of ALL my problems.

I didn't flip a car, end up in jail, or kill somebody (all things, by the way, that happened to people I know who used to drink the way I did). But I had finally found my line, and I had crossed it big time. Being a fantastic mom is central to my life, and there was no fucking way I was ever going to let my kids down like that again.

I.

WAS.

DONE.

## How's It Going for You?

Deciding whether you want to keep drinking, cut back, or quit completely—especially in our society, where alcohol is often equated with everything fun—can be confusing. Figuring out if there's actually an issue to address or you're making a big deal out of nothing can make that decision even more fraught with anxiety. And determining how the status of your stuck life and your drinking are somehow connected? Well, that can seem downright impossible.

I want you to know that it's okay to be unsure about all that. You don't have to admit to, commit to, or decide anything right now. All I'm asking is that you keep an open mind—and keep reading until you get clear on what's been holding you back and have a plan for moving forward.

In the first part of this book, you're going to assess whether your relationship with alcohol is truly the kind of problem you have an inkling it might be, and how that connects to any pain, dissatisfaction, and unhappiness you might be experiencing. You'll look at how your environment and mental health may be exacerbating the situation and address that, too.

In the second part of the book, you'll discover other ways to take the edge off that won't leave you hungover and depressed and learn how to handle those inevitable situations where you're being offered unwanted drinks or that make you want to drink heavily. (Holidays with the family, anyone?) Consider this your short-term triage plan—a way to get started. The goal here is to get you set up for success. It's a veritable *do this, not that* survival guide!

Right here is where other books and programs stop—but not this one. I didn't stop drinking only to live a small life. That would have felt like going backward into what I started drinking to escape in the first place. I wanted a life so rich, so rewarding, and so meaningful that alcohol was a complete non-issue. Don't you want that, too? Of course you do!

That's why the third part of this book focuses on designing your new and improved life from the ground up. In it, you'll envision the exact way you dream of living but never really thought possible. You'll replace those tired old stories you've been telling yourself for who-knows-how-long with new spiritual laws, bringing light and joy back into your everyday existence and making you a blessing in other people's lives. Finally, you'll work on forgiveness and letting go so you can live and love freely again. While you work through understanding and applying these spiritual laws to your daily life, your life will transform into a rich experience of light, hope, and energy, with relationships in which you belong and an edge to your career that propels you beyond your current reality.

By the time you finish this book, you'll have the confidence to take decisive action because you'll finally have that clarity you've been seeking. You'll be armed with practical tools and a new spiritual approach that are immediately applicable to every domain of your life. You'll have a clear picture of your ideal future self and know how to start living like her TODAY.

And you'll also know an easier and more inviting way to lose the booze if and when you decide it's time.

## Where I Went from There

After my awful birthday debacle, I actually ended up going to one of "those" meetings. It was ten in the morning on a Thursday, the day before I turned forty (in my typical overachiever fashion, I'd scheduled my party the weekend before my actual birthday). The people there were exactly the kind of people you'd expect to be free at ten on a Thursday morning, and they scared the living hell out of me. As I nervously looked for a seat, this woman glanced up at me and commented, "Nobody walks through these doors by mistake." I metaphorically ran out of there shrieking.

The whole scene only served to reinforce my story that being alcohol-free was going to suck. *If this is going to be my social milieu,* I thought, *then sobriety is going to be miserable.* There I was: Kay Kay Career Girl, wearing a business suit with a blouse tied at the neck in a floppy bow. I was carrying a briefcase. I had a big-time job. These people seemed more like the under-the-bridge cirrhosis of the liver guys, and I wasn't sure who, if anyone, would employ them.

Do I sound judge-y and insecure? That's because I was. Appearances were so important to me back then. That's all that mattered. I thought that having alcohol problems was a failure, and to me, at the time, those people looked like total failures.

I tried another meeting in another grungy little building. This one was even more terrifying than the last, if that's possible. The room was thick with cigarette smoke. The group was composed of more bedraggled, bewildered-looking old men sipping endless cups of burnt, bitter, black coffee from white, spongy, non-eco-friendly

Styrofoam cups. It was absolutely nothing I could relate to—or ever WANTED to relate to.

Luckily, one of the only other women there gave me a tip on yet another meeting that might be a better fit for me. It was only half a block away, so off I went yet again. Jackpot! I was greeted there by other well-dressed career women who all seemed to be carrying Louis Vuitton bags. I needed an outward sign that I was going to be okay, and that was it for me. They looked like my outward definition of success, seemed genuinely excited to welcome me into their group, and I could imagine them becoming my friends.

More than anything, though, those women seemed HAPPY. I thought, *if it works for them, then maybe it'll work for me. Maybe I haven't completely ruined my life just yet.*

(A little P.S. here to try to redeem myself: by going to those meetings—no matter where, when, and who the attendees were—I learned to listen to people's stories and find the connection regardless of the external details. I found out it wasn't about how someone looked, where they lived, or what kind of bag they carried, it was about how their story struck a chord with me. As a result, I ended up making dear friends with all kinds of people, friendships that might look unlikely to the outside, but friendships that are deep and heartfelt. After I lost the alcohol and started working on myself, my insecurities rapidly diminished and appearances no longer drove my definition of success.)

## Where Do YOU Want to Go from Here?

Hint: It doesn't have to be where I went (unless you want to, in which case, I totally, wholeheartedly encourage you to go for it). Maybe you just want to be Juicy AF (alcohol-free, of course!). Either way, I invite you to stop the drinking spiral.

Before we dive any further into what that means and how it's going to change your life so much for the better, I first want to note that I have the utmost respect, gratitude, and reverence for the program that got me to finally stop drinking. I have the biggest appreciation for those women who greeted me with such enthusiasm and supported me every step of the way. They had a profound effect on my life, and I would not be here today—or the person I am today—without them.

And yet. There's always something, right?

That program was created by white professional men. It was created FOR people just like them. And they often have egos so gigantic that puncturing those humongous, inflated egos is probably a very necessary path to recovery.

Most women aren't coming from that place. Our egos are usually well in check. In fact, too many of us ALREADY feel like there's something existentially wrong with who we are, so there's zero need for anyone to bring us down any further.

At least for me, being told *you are flawed* and *you drink because you're not only flawed but also selfish* and *oh, by the way, you should keep track of how flawed and selfish you are every day* just wasn't something I wanted or needed to hear, especially so often. It didn't seem very motivating. It certainly wasn't uplifting or healing of my existential primary fault line of feeling like "not enough."

Besides, all that talking about not drinking made it so I was actually spending a lot of time thinking about drinking. As novelist Fyodor Dostoevsky once said, "Try to pose for yourself this task: not to think of a polar bear, and you will see that the cursed thing will come to mind every minute." (And now I'm going to be thinking about polar bears all day.) My goal was a life where I didn't HAVE to think about drinking anymore because I was having so much more fun and success NOT drinking.

In meetings, they always say, "*Take what you need and leave the rest,*" so that's exactly what I did. Applying my deep knowledge in the areas of personal development and spirituality, I adapted, updated, and "joy-ified" the program so that it spoke directly to women. I then tested, improved, and perfected this new approach with the women I've been mentoring for the past twenty years. I've seen firsthand how effective, motivating, and powerful this method is, whether used as an adjunct to another program or on its own.

Based on that long-term success, I launched Juicy AF—a community of like-minded, accomplished women supporting each other in living their best alcohol-free lives. In Juicy AF, there's no torturing yourself or feeling like you're going without. No self-flagellation, self-doubt, or self-hatred. Instead, there's a lot of joyful spiritual substitution. It's all about *What can I do instead of drinking, and how can I make that as fun and meaningful as possible?*

Juicy AF is based in positivity. It's effervescent. It's sparkly. It downright glitters. And it works like magic as long as you put in the work (which, may I remind you, is FUN). Sound good?

I'll answer that one for you: it sounds fucking **GREAT**.

## Where I Am Now

Juicy AF is literally my reason for being these days. I know this is what I was put on earth to do. And I am positively giddy about the giant impact it is having on so many women's lives, all of whom were once in the exact same spot you're in right now.

Today, I'm the person I wanted to become when I drank. Back then, I thought drinking was making my life more exciting and adventurous when it was actually making it smaller and more monotonous. Without alcohol ruling my life, everything is so much bigger and better, more meaningful and connected than I ever imagined it could be.

Alcohol was an anchor dragging me below baseline. I invested a LOT of energy every day just to get back to functioning well. Now that the anchor line has been severed, the same amount of energy has propelled me into a pretty magical life. I've had leaps and bounds more career, professional, and financial success sober, even though

I was so desperate for those kinds of accomplishments when I was drinking. (Not to brag, but my relationship with money and how much more I made once I was sober is absolutely STAGGERING.)

I've launched four successful businesses. I've consulted with Fortune 200 companies, enabling them to generate—literally—billions in new revenue. I am happily married to a guy that people always remark is such a good man, unlike those terrible people I used to date. And I'm an executive coach, ordained minister, and clairvoyant healer with twenty-plus fabulously juicy years of sobriety under my belt, not someone slowly withering away at a desk, buried under a pile of corporate bullshit, slamming back vodkas by the dozen.

I'm finally comfortable in my own skin. I've found the tribe where I belong. I'm no longer trying to pretend about anything. I simply don't have to pretend anymore, because I'm very clear about who I am, what I'm good at, and what I suck at (which I never could have admitted before I got sober, because sucking doesn't fit with pretending).

Best of all, I'm truly excited about my life. I've constructed it to make me happy rather than to impress somebody else. It is idiosyncratic—like I am—and fits me perfectly.

## Where We Are Now

In America alone, there are more than twelve million people who have a fraught relationship with alcohol. It is truly an epidemic. So welcome to the club nobody wants to be in and so many are, I guess.

And yet. There's always something. Again.

I invite you to be hopeful that a Juicy AF life can be both FULL and FUN. That it doesn't have to mean constantly craving or missing something. That it makes dumping the booze feel like the best decision on the planet. I'm living proof of the truth of all that.

In fact, I want you to consider this entire book an invitation. To experiment and play with choices, ideas, and behaviors. To reconnect with your intuition and spirit. To open yourself up to possibilities you can't even see from where you're sitting right now. To join a community of like-minded women who make you feel supported and understood. You'll learn so much about yourself and what your life can become, along with some practical, down-to-earth, enjoyable, immediately useful tools that make losing the booze easier if that's what you decide to do.

Don't worry: I'm not going to suddenly hit you with dogma once you start turning more pages. You won't be made to feel powerless or like a victim. I'm not coming from any specific religious angle. There's no cult you have to join or any kind of public admission required. It's a book, not brain surgery. Try out what I suggest. Keep doing what works and ignore the rest.

I know thinking about ditching alcohol can be incredibly hard when every domain of life from vacations to family gatherings to dating to friendship seems to revolve around it. Drinking is normalized in our culture, and I don't expect that to change any time soon. But I do hope realizing there are other awesome, accomplished women living much bigger lives without alcohol—who are waiting to welcome you into the Juicy AF community—gives you hope that you can enjoy the same kind of transformation in your life.

Things CAN be different this time. They WILL be. The sooner you start making changes, the sooner your life will start changing for the better.

If you're thinking right now, *this better be way more fun than margaritas with the girls or I'm out of here,* then you're in luck. It is, by miles. Your Juicy AF journey starts right here, right now.

LFG!

---

- *Sober curious? Start with Part One of this book to assess your drinking and give you clarity on how to move forward.*

- *Struggling to get sober? Skip directly to Part Two, your short-term triage plan for putting down the booze and picking up your life. Then, keep reading Part Three to develop your long-term Juicy AF life plan.*
- *Sober and bored AF? Skip right to Part Three and start envisioning your dream life right into reality, starting right now.*

---

# PART ONE

# Something's Not Right

Is Juicy AF the answer?

## CHAPTER ONE

# Is This REALLY a Problem?

TOWARD THE END of my ill-fated affair with alcohol, I started dating a guy who was sixteen years sober. It was a big leap for me, because I generally only dated men who drank as much or more than I did. He was married, which I guess was part of the dysfunctional allure, but I'm actually grateful we got together because he ended up being very helpful on my journey to sobriety.

One time, I remember asking him, "How do you know if you ACTUALLY have a problem?" He told me if I was drinking before I went to parties, it was a big red flag. I didn't do that—unlikely as it might sound, I wasn't into pre-gaming—so I felt like I was still probably somewhat okay. Ish.

I also wasn't drinking every day, which I took as another sign that my drinking couldn't possibly have been too terribly problematic. Thursday nights were usually my starting point, which would then of course roll right into Friday and Saturday nights. And maybe I'd have a couple of mimosas or Bloody Marys at Sunday brunch. Oh, and there were sometimes events I had to attend on Mondays, Tuesdays and/or Wednesdays where drinks were part of the equation. Okay, fine, even I had to admit to myself that despite my best intentions, alcohol had a sneaky way of creeping into other days of the week.

But it's not like I NEEDED it. I didn't drink in the morning (well, except for the occasional boozy Sunday brunch). My body wasn't going to go into the DTs without it. I wasn't someone who'd have to check themselves into a hospital if I ever decided to stop drinking or else I'd die. *See?* I told myself. *Definitely not a problem.* I figured all I needed to do was tweak my habits and slow my roll a little.

So I resolved not to have wine in the house anymore. If it was there, I knew it would start calling to me, *KayKay, come get me!* And I also knew I was undoubtedly going to answer that call. I got rid of my entire stash of vino.

I felt so virtuous watching my former BFF swirl around and then disappear down the drain. Free at last! And yet "somehow," I always found myself at the nearest convenience store buying wine every night after work. I was disappointed in my lack of willpower but figured at least I wasn't making it so easy on myself anymore, and maybe tomorrow I wouldn't make that same stop on my way home. That must be worth something, right?

Then I decided if I was still going to drink wine—which I clearly was, as much as ever—I was going to make myself drink a glass of water between every glass of wine. As you might imagine, that only ever lasted until the second glass of wine. I ended up being only slightly more hydrated and no less hungover.

I made a rule that I was only going to drink on certain nights. That worked well—until, of course, I'd find myself out with people drinking margaritas on a Wednesday when I was only supposed to be drinking on Fridays. The negotiation in my head would immediately start: *Should I make an exception to the rule?* The answer to that one was always yes, too.

Finally, I thought, *I'll just limit myself to two glasses of wine on the days I choose to drink.* Since we've already established that my off switch no longer existed, that one was pure, unadulterated wishful thinking. My body and biology don't work that way. I couldn't do it (although sometimes, very occasionally, I actually COULD, which made my whole struggle that much more confounding).

To my shock and dismay, my very definitely non-problem-drinking wasn't listening to my rules. It didn't fucking care what I said. What disrespect!

It felt like I had fallen under a magic spell of the not-so-magical variety, which was the weirdest and most disconcerting experience in the entire world.

## Booze Doesn't Care About Rules

My goal was simple: to find a way to drink less. The only problem was, there was no such thing as moderation for me anymore. My off switch had gotten uninstalled, and it wasn't ever getting reinstalled. (Actually, now that I think about it, that equipment had probably never existed in the first place for me. I was born without an off switch!)

My body metabolizes alcohol differently than other people's bodies do. It's simply my biology, and there's nothing I can do to change that. At no point was I somehow going to magically say, "I had half a glass of wine. I'm done now."

Besides, if I was being really honest with myself, moderation wasn't REALLY what I wanted. What I wanted was to drink as much as always, only without feeling like shit the next day or having to face any negative consequences. Too bad that's not a thing.

I wasn't drinking because it tasted so good with my dinner, I drank because I wanted to take the edge off. Get drunk. Be numb. Go a little wild. And while those ARE things, they are very fleeting. None had anywhere near the staying power my next-day regret and remorse did. It was never a fair fight in the first place.

Researchers at Cornell University estimate we make up to 35,000 decisions a day. That's a lot of deciding, which gets tiring—and a tired Decider does not make good choices. This explains why we're much more likely to eat a healthy breakfast than a healthy dinner, or why dinner on Monday is plain chicken breast with a side of broccoli and by Friday it's an entire pizza washed down with a pitcher of beer. When our brains are exhausted, our vigilance erodes.

So of course my rules didn't work! All they did was make me think constantly about whether I was going to drink or not. I was always wondering whether I should make an exception to whatever boundary I had tried to apply that day. Exceptions BECAME my rules because my Decider was overloaded, and my vigilance went kaput.

And yet. (Again with the "and yets.")

It's easier to make a 100 percent commitment than a 99 percent or less one. As Clayton Christensen, former Harvard Business School professor said in his book *How Will You Measure Your Life?*, "It's easier to hold your principles 100 percent of the time than it is to hold them 98 percent of the time." That's because a 100 percent commitment is only ONE decision. Anything else requires a constant assessment: *Is this an exception? Or that? Or this?* All that back and forth tires out our Deciders—and tired Deciders go with what feels good in the moment rather than the intention they set previously.

With rules, there's always wiggle room, and boy, did I learn to wiggle well. My thinking was, *I'm just going to try. Oops, I tried, but it didn't work. Oh, well, I guess I'll try something else.* It was a never-ending spiral eerily similar to the drinking-remorse-drinking spiral that had taken up more than half of my life by this point.

Which I fell right back into after the rules failed, of course. I thought making rules would make me feel better, but trying and failing at those rules only made me feel like shit. So I drank to make myself feel better. And then I felt like worse shit.

And so the cycle just continued until I finally made a 100 percent commitment and stopped that spiral forever.

## Quiz: Five Questions to Clarity (Plus a Bonus Clarifier)

So far, I've shared a lot of the not-so-pretty details about my former drinking life. Now I want to know more about what's going on with you.

My darling, I invite you to participate in the experience I outline below. Here's a quiz to help you get a better handle on whether your drinking habits are truly problematic. Be super honest with your answers here. I'm not your doctor, I'm not a cop, and I'm not your disapproving partner. No one needs to know but you. It's no one else's business but your own.

You came here looking for clarity, right? This is your chance. Go on now.

1.  Of the last five times you drank, how many times did you end up more or less wildly drunk?
    a. 5
    b. 4
    c. 3
    d. 1 or 2
    e. 0

2.  When you drink, how often do you do things that you would never do sober?
    a. Always
    b. Most of the time
    c. Half the time
    d. Occasionally
    e. Never

3.  Most of the time when you start drinking, how strong is your desire for more alcohol?
    a. It possesses me

b. It's pretty strong

c. Sometimes I want more, sometimes I stop

d. I can resist the urge to keep drinking

e. I don't have a desire to keep drinking

4. The past ten times you've been drinking, how many times did you say *never again*, only to start drinking again?

   a. 9–10

   b. 6–8

   c. 5

   d. 1–4

   e. 0

5. If someone followed you for a week, every moment, would you be proud of what they saw?

   a. Not at all

   b. Not really

   c. I'd be okay

   d. Somewhat

   e. Absolutely

6. Thinking about your life overall, do you feel it is heading in the right direction?

   a. Yes

   b. No

Okay, time to score your test. Anytime you answered A through D in questions one through five, I want you to give yourself one point. E's are worth zero points.

Are you done adding it all up? Okay, great. Now here's that clarity you wanted.

If you have any points at all—even just one of them—your drinking is indeed a problem. And if in the last question you said your life is not heading in the right direction, your drinking is likely a big part of why that is.

Honestly, that's the best news I can imagine giving you. Seriously. You can't address something that you're blind to or kidding yourself about, and now you know for sure.

If you scored a zero, this is the one and only time in your life you've probably been psyched you failed a test. Keep reading anyhow. You'll still learn lots of ways to improve your life regardless of your results.


## Wait, WHAT?

If you scored one or three or five points, you might be thinking to yourself, *Those quiz results CAN'T be right. Alcoholics are mostly guys, right? They're bums wearing trench coats and drinking out of bags. That's not me at all. I'm well-educated. I have a great job, great friends, and great family. I care about what I look like. I work out. Ask anyone who knows me, and they'll tell you, "She's a cool, nice, together person. No way she has a problem!"*

I know. I KNOW. I get it.

You're NOT the classic stereotype of someone with alcohol issues. But neither am I, and neither are the women in the Juicy AF community. None of us has ever been a trench-coat-wearing, bag-drinking bum. We weren't falling down drunk every single night. We didn't start drinking again first thing every morning.

In fact, we're very smart and have great achievements. One of the Juicy AF members is the head of fundraising for a global organization. Another is an occupational therapist. Yet another is a provost of a university. One has her Ph.D. in the middle atmosphere. (Who even knew there WAS such an interesting, brainy specialty?)

Honestly, someone with alcohol problems is USUALLY not who you'd expect. It's someone like me. It's the multi-talented, extremely accomplished women in the Juicy AF community. And now you know that it's you, too.

There's no need to label yourself as an alcoholic. You can choose to say you're Juicy AF, or that your status right now is AF. But quite frankly, why put a label on it at all? It's not necessary for moving forward.

My guess is you might be feeling shocked, upset, angry, like you just had the carpet pulled out from under you, or all of the above right now. That's okay. It's just called being human.

## So NOW What?

You're probably also saying to yourself, *I can't imagine my life without alcohol, and you just made me realize alcohol is the root of all my problems. What am I supposed to do now?*

The answer to that is simple: Now you stop drinking.

One hundred percent commitment to being alcohol-free is the only way forward. I want to be very clear here: The answer is NOT that you haven't created the right rule yet. Any rule that still includes drinking alcohol in any amount at all, ever, will not work. Haven't you already proved that to yourself time and again?

If your body reacts to alcohol the way mine does, you can't control how much you drink once you start. It's a biological phenomenon. Switching from vodka to hard cider isn't going to matter. Only drinking on Tuesdays? Not gonna matter. Only drinking at home. Never drinking at home. None. Of. It. Works.

The fact that rules and moderation will forever fail you is more good news. Really, it is. Because let's face it, right now you're doing things drunk that you would never do sober. I used to believe being drunk was a "get out of jail free" card, and that I didn't have to feel bad about a particular action I took when I was drunk because I clearly wouldn't have done it if I was sober. I thought what Drunk Me did didn't count.

Oh, but it does. That's still YOU. Whatever you're doing when you're drunk still counts as what YOU'RE doing. And is that really the person you want to be? Because as long as you're still drinking, that's the person you ARE. If that is a horrifying thought, not drinking is the only answer. Period. End of story.

So here's my challenge to you: Make a commitment to not drink and stick to it. Even if that's just *I'm not going to drink for thirty days* to start. I'm going to be right here cheering you on and helping you figure out exactly how to do just that.

So let's get going. No time like the present. As the ancient Chinese philosopher, Lao Tzu once said, "The journey of a thousand miles begins with a single step."

> **Ready to do this thing? Post on your social media #100committedaf and tag @jucy_af_life. I'll be there cheering you on!**

## You Can't Fight Biology

Willpower is a wuss. Your mind will never win out over your biology. Once you lose your off switch, it is NEVER coming back.

You now have clarity that your body doesn't metabolize or interact with alcohol the way other people's bodies do. It has an abnormal response to a specific substance. You can learn how to deal with that fact—by not putting that substance into your body anymore—but you can't change it. That is simply your biology.

I get canker sores when I eat sugar, which is honestly the most infuriating thing. Twelve hours after a few bites of lava cake, I have a sore in my mouth. I don't want it to be that way, but after learning my lesson time and again, I fundamentally know this is what my body does.

So then I had to decide what I wanted to do with that information. I knew if I really wanted a piece of lava cake, I could go ahead and eat it and the result would be a canker sore the next day. So my choice was to not eat sugar anymore, because I decided the pain simply wasn't worth it. (I did choose to eat cake at my son's wedding. And yes, my body did its thing the next day.)

In the same way my body can't deal with sugar, the way our bodies react to alcohol is not our fault. It can't be solved with more determination and willpower. It's not a moral failing. It doesn't make us bad people.

And now you get to choose to stop fighting it, because the pain is not worth it.

---

## BREAKOUT EXERCISE: COST-BENEFIT ANALYSIS

*Lest you think that going AF means losing something that actually ADDS value to your life, let's do a cost-benefit analysis of your drinking. Take out a piece of paper and draw a line down the middle of it. Ready? Okay.*

*In the first column, write down the benefits of alcohol. What do you get from it? Clearly, you wouldn't still be doing it if it weren't working for you on some level.*

*When I did this exercise, first on my list was that I felt more comfortable in my skin when I drank. I thought it made me wittier. Prettier. Outrageously funny. It was like alcohol gave me a temporary persona to borrow.*

*Next, write down the disadvantages of your drinking in the opposite column. What does it cost you? You must realize there's a downside or you wouldn't be reading this book.*

*I was shocked to discover that drinking for me was a Faustian bargain. Once the alcohol was out of my system, I always ended up feeling far worse in my skin. Which meant the payment for it was my soul.*

*Now take a good, long look at your list. What do you notice? What patterns do you see? This is not about which side is longer.*

*If you're at a loss, here's a hint: There's probably a temporal element to it. The things on the "good" side of the list are generally short-lived, like my witty-pretty-outrageous-funny persona. And—this is a big and—not only that, but they have long-term shitty consequences. For some people, that might be a DUI or a cracked-up car. In my case, it was more like my self-respect. My integrity. My physical well-being.*

*So now the question becomes: What's lasting and what's fleeting? And which is most important to you?*

*I bet you already suspected the answer to that one. And now once again, you know for sure.*

# PART TWO

# No Booze, No Problem!

A short-term triage plan
for becoming Juicy AF

# CHAPTER TWO

---

# Triggers and How to Deal with Them

I GOT MARRIED VERY YOUNG and had kids very young. I got divorced very young, too. My first husband and I weren't a great match to begin with, and by a certain point we were barely limping along.

We were still stuck living in that unhappy limbo when I came home from work one night to an untenable situation: My one-year-old hadn't been cared for, and my six-year-old had barricaded herself in her room because she was scared. I took one look around and was just like, *fuck this, I'm done.* (Very on-brand for me at the time.) I packed a single suitcase for the three of us, grabbed my kids, and left.

My sudden departure was largely unplanned and definitely dramatic, which I tended to be at the time. Nothing about it was deliberate. In fact, the only thing I had done in advance was hire an attorney. No actual wheels had been set in motion. When you're addicted, there's something insidious that happens inside your brain. It makes you start acting like someone you don't even recognize, so it's no surprise that the way I went about ending my marriage was not the way a sane, grounded, orderly person would.

In the middle of all this chaos, my parents had moved from the nearby suburbs to Florida. Bad timing. No more trusted, familial babysitters for me. I was left without a soft place to land.

With nowhere else to go, my company had to put us up in temporary housing. Suddenly, everything was different. The alarm clock was different. The towels were different. My daughter's school was different. The commute was different. I basically had to rebuild our lives from the ground up—which was ironic, because there was absolutely no grounding in my life whatsoever.

Abject terror became my predominant emotion. I was scared I was going to lose custody of my kids. I was scared I was going to lose my job. I was so scared about money, I'd buy one Lean Cuisine and split it between the three of us.

I'd work, work, work, come home, take care of the kids and whatever legal thing regarding the separation awaited me, and then get up the next morning and do it all again. By Thursday nights, it was always like, *oh my God, I am absolutely flattened.* Of course, a glass of wine seemed like the perfect antidote to all that stress. Instead of just going to bed, I'd start drinking.

I'd have a glass of wine with dinner. Then I'd put the kids to bed, finish that bottle, and open the next. I never knew how much of the second bottle would be left by the time I put MYSELF to bed.

I was now living #singlemomlife. That is, until the kids went to their dad's every other weekend. Then I'd quickly morph into a single, flirty thirty-something and go hit up all the street fairs, bars, and dance clubs the city had to offer. I was living two entirely different lives: Career-Driven Working Mom during the week, and Crazy Party Girl on alternating weekends. It was like high school all over again.

Despite all the behind-the-scenes drama going on in my life, I'd always managed to maintain an extremely professional persona at work up until now. Suddenly, though, my personal and professional worlds were starting to collide. This did not bode well for my career or my life in general.

Case in point: I found out my favorite drinking buddy's other best buddy—who always seemed to be at the same bars at the same time we were, and saw me out of my mind, all of the time—worked for my biggest client. It nearly killed me knowing that my client was just a single degree of Kevin Bacon away from finding out about my double life. I worried myself sick over it.

And this: as an assistant account executive for a popular beer brand, it was my job to entertain the client. In the advertising world, that was always code for "take them out drinking." One night, I was so drunk I fell down on the dance floor while dancing with the beer brand's Senior VP. I FELL DOWN. Who the fuck does that?

And this: At a work conference, I noticed one of my friends had only finished half the glass of wine she ordered with dinner. As we were all getting up to leave the table, I turned back around and slammed it. Because wine is a terrible thing to waste, right?

So there I was: ambitious and successful yet overcommitted, exhausted, and frantic all the time. Everything in my life was high drama. Drinking was my conditioned response, my attempt to combat all that.

It was something so habitual, yet I was absolutely blind to it even as it became interwoven into the fabric of my daily life. I didn't even think about it. Like, when was the last time you thought about the R key on your keyboard? You don't think about it until it doesn't work. (Oh, hi there, little R key. I see you now.)

I recently read this really interesting book called *Never Enough* (it is fucking brilliant, BTW). The author, Judith Geisel, is a recovering heroin addict who is now a leading scientist on the topic of the neuropsychology of addiction. In the book she talks a lot about homeostasis within our bodies, and how that changes based on what the body experiences on a regular basis.

For example, our bodies are constantly working to maintain a consistent body temperature. Whenever we're exposed to cold, our brain receives a signal that we need to produce more heat and we start to shiver. Shivering effectively works to bring heat back into the body and maintain the correct temperature.

The same thing happens with alcohol—when you drink a lot, the body adjusts. Because drinking relaxes and calms the body, the body starts to create the opposite—getting all keyed up (read: anxious)—until you have another drink (and there's that spiral in the making). Drinking more and more is required to ease the ratcheting up of anxiety we experience. Not drinking requires our bodies to adjust again and find a NEW homeostasis. It takes a while to make that adjustment. It will happen, but it's not going to be instantaneous.

Applying the homeostasis theory to my drinking: back then I thought I drank in response to the stressors in my life. What I think now is that because I was addicted to alcohol, I unconsciously CREATED all that drama to make it seem like the reason I "needed" a drink was not the real reason at all.

In reality, what I thought was the answer to my problems actually WAS my problem.

## Identifying Your Triggers

For me, Thursday night was always a trigger to start drinking. My drinking buddy was a trigger. Work events, another trigger. I was constantly being triggered—which meant I was also constantly drinking.

Being so far removed from that reality now, I realize that EVERYTHING I chose back then revolved around alcohol. I worked in advertising, which is a boozy profession. I always went out with friends who liked to drink as much as I did. When I started dating my ex-husband, the first thing he invited me to was a cocktail party.

I was eighteen years old at the time and he was thirty-seven, so that offer seemed incredibly sophisticated and exciting.

Something I loved about his family was the way they drank, and how often. Whenever we'd travel with his mom, she would always pack bottles of gin, vodka, and Canadian Club in her suitcase. In her opinion, buying drinks at a bar was a waste of money. So before dinner, we'd all gather in her hotel room and have a cocktail, and afterwards we'd always go back for a nightcap of Canadian Club. At the time, I thought that was pure genius.

Once I was even going on vacation with a girlfriend to Glacier, Montana. I assumed there would be no good wine in a place that remote, so I decided weeks in advance I'd just have to drink vodka instead. What type of alcohol I was going to drink on vacation was baked into my trip planning, that's how ubiquitous it had become in my life!

How much of your life is arranged around alcohol right now? And how are you going to change that?

## Deactivating the Trigger

As we've already found out, willpower is a wimp. You can't get to your sparkly future on willpower. To get set up for success, you'll need to address your physical space, psychology, and social structures.

You're going to have to make some changes to the way you normally do things. Some of these will be temporary. Some will be forever.

First up: an environmental audit. Get a notebook and a pen or take your phone out. Make a list or video of everything in your living and working space that triggers a habitual drinking response. That might include wine glasses, champagne flutes, or beer steins. Corkscrews and openers. The giant tumbler emblazoned with *Mommy's sippy cup*. Plaques that read *It's wine o'clock!* And most definitely your stash of booze.

Now, ask a friend to come over and help you get rid of it all. Donate whatever you can. Pour out all your booze. Trash the rest. Get rid of the reminders.

Next, do a social audit. List who you hang out with and what you do with them. Is drinking embedded into your relationship? Do you do any activities that aren't centered around alcohol? If not, you might have to put those drinking buddies on hold for a few weeks or months while you're trying to navigate being newly sober.

Next, check your social media. Delete all accounts that glorify drinking and debauchery. Start following sober curious and sober accounts. Populate your feed so it goes in a new and healthier direction.

Finally, do a mental health audit. The best way is by making an appointment with a professional who can assess whether you have depression, trauma, anxiety disorder, bipolar, or anything else going on that could be one of the reasons you're drinking so much.

When I first took this step, I was diagnosed with depression. I wasn't surprised. It explained why I always felt like I was submerged under water and had to paddle really hard just to get the tip of my nose out for a quick breath.

Once my depression was being treated, it made a world of difference in my mood and ability to deal with life without drinking. I didn't have to "rise and grind" anymore because I woke up feeling energetic and positive naturally. All the energy I used to expend simply trying to catch a breath was now being funneled into having an incredible life. Once I was freed up like that, my career took off like a rocket.

Later, I was also diagnosed as being bipolar, which explains why drinking had been so self-medicating for me. It numbed me, and numb isn't up and it isn't down. Without drinking, my thoughts used to get spun up like a hamster on speed on a hamster wheel. My mind raced. I'd wonder why everybody else couldn't just hurry the fuck up. Alcohol was the only thing that could shut my brain up for a minute. Treating the bipolar symptoms stopped those racing thoughts in their tracks and sent that hamster packing.

Please don't skip this part, no matter how tempting it might seem. It's more likely than not that you will get a diagnosis, because the comorbidity of mental health problems and alcohol abuse is staggering. In fact, the National Council on Drug Abuse reports that at least 50 percent of women with substance abuse issues have concurrent mental health issues.

Once you have clarity, go get therapy for that trauma, depression, anxiety, or whatever it is that has been hiding below the surface of your drinking. If you've been unknowingly self-medicating with alcohol, your mental health issues are going to come roaring to the surface when you take away that self-medication. Stopping the drinking spiral is fantastic, but it is not going to heal or help with any of that.

Mental health and addiction are related, but they really are two different things and each needs to be addressed separately.

## Make a New Plan (Stan)

Now the question becomes: What can you do instead of reacting to your trigger with drinking? That vacuum needs to be filled and the path of least resistance is going to be doing what you've always done. It's a matter of being prepared.

This is where joyful substitution starts to come into play. Doing something pleasurable that makes you happy but ISN'T drinking is the key. Can you hit the gym or get a massage instead of going out with your drinking buddy? Can you read a book or talk to an AF friend? What about just walking around the block a few times?

Twenty minutes can make all the difference between staying committed and giving in.

You may have to avoid seeing that friend you always went to happy hour with before, and you may have to drive a different way home so you don't "accidentally" turn into the parking lot of your favorite beer garden. Speaking of which, did you know you can set location-based reminders on your phone? That way, whenever you're in the vicinity of your favorite liquor store or the bar, your phone delivers a message to you from yourself saying, *Hey, dumb shit. Don't do it.* Works for me.

I also want to encourage you to lean on a sober buddy for support. There's no way I could've gotten and stayed AF for as long and as happily as I have been by simply reading a book or taking a program. Community matters most. That's the antidote.

There are a lot of places sober people collect beyond just the top-of-mind meetings (which, as you already know, I absolutely recommend if that's something you want to do). You can easily find an online tribe that's trying to do the same thing you are. There's a subreddit called Stop Drinking that has more than 352,000 members—there's bound to be someone in there you vibe with and feel connected to. There's Smart Recovery and Women for Recovery, both online groups for AF women. There's my Juicy AF community, which is also for women only. There's a Sober Squad Facebook group for Peloton users.

Just start Googling. You'll figure it out.

Old habits die hard, and it takes more energy to do something different than it does to just do the same thing you've always done. So write your awesome substitution plan down on paper. Put it in your calendar. Program those location-based messages into your phone.

Make a commitment to do something different while your Decider is still fresh.

## Short-Term Fixes, Long-Term Growth

So this is how we kick things off—with baby steps. It's like starting a diet: You're tossing out all the junk food in the house and committing to not buying it or eating it anymore. Now whenever you want a chocolate bar, you have a plan to eat an apple instead and you have the apple with you. The longer you give yourself a break from junk food—or booze, as the case may be—the more likely you are to be able to live comfortably without it.

Basically, what you just did was create a crisis intervention plan for yourself. The National Institute on Drug Abuse reports that people who stay in rehab or sober living for longer amounts of time have much higher rates of recovery than people who only do twenty-eight-day programs. So give it some time. Give yourself a chance. Let it take root.

Like the saying goes, take it one day at a time. Or if a day feels too long, back up your mental time horizons until it feels doable. Can you manage to make it until bedtime without picking up? Can you go the next ten minutes without having a drink? Can you take your next breath without having one?

Keep telling yourself, *Oh, I can drink tomorrow.* Tomorrow is always tomorrow, you know? It's never going to be tomorrow.

Tell yourself you're going to give this a shot for thirty or sixty days before assessing what effect it has had. When that day comes, you can ask yourself whether life has gotten better AF. My guess is the answer will be yes—by miles.

After I did this—and kept on doing it for the past twenty-some-odd years—my once chaotic, dramatic, anxious, exhausted, stalled-out life now looks like this: I work on my own schedule. I know how to manage my moods. I know how to differentiate what's my stuff and everybody else's stuff. I'm married to a guy that I absolutely adore. I laugh a lot with my kids. I live in my dream town in the mountains. I'm surrounded by a pine forest. I drive a sports car. My mom chose to live close to me in her elderly years. I've traveled around the world. I've started four companies. This is my second book.

And yet ditching the booze is STILL the single best thing I've ever done. In short, my sober life is rich. Rewarding. Stimulating. I have relationships that are fun and playful—for real. I've seen and experienced some of the most fascinating things life has to offer.

My AF life is incredible, and I just know yours will be, too. Give yourself a chance to see how you shine.

---

## BREAKOUT EXERCISE:
## IDENTIFYING YOUR TRIGGERS

*I imagine there are things that have you set on automatic pilot as well—situations that make you immediately think* Time to drink! *If you don't know exactly what they are, no worries. Let's find out together.*

*Get out another piece of paper and make three columns. Ready? Great.*

*Think about the last time you drank. In the first column, write down the reason why you started drinking. In the next column, write down what happened. In the last column, write whether it worked.*

*Do this for as many instances as you can remember. Go back in time chronologically. Be as specific as you can.*

*For example, you might write:* I was at a bar with a beer client, so I started drinking because that's just what you do in advertising when you entertain anyone, but especially with an alcohol brand. What happened next was I fell down while dancing with a Senior VP. No, it didn't work well. *(Oh, wait, that was me.)*

*Now take a look at your answers. What kinds of patterns are you starting to see? Are there specific times, places, and people that "make" you want to drink? What emotional states crop up time and time again?*

*When I did this exercise, what I realized was I drank because booze was there. That was it, plain and simple. It would never have occurred to me to be around alcohol and drink something else—that's how much of an automated behavior it was.*

*Once you know what your triggers are, make a plan to untrigger yourself. Being aware and prepared are your keys to success here. You've got this!*

---

# CHAPTER THREE

# How to Not Drink (When It Seems Like Everyone Else Is)

ONCE, REALLY EARLY ON in my sobriety, I ran into my secretary at one of "those" meetings and was completely mortified. I wanted to find an escape hatch but of course there wasn't one. As someone new to the Juicy AF lifestyle, it didn't occur to me that *hey, she's here too, we're both in the same boat.*

Four months later, I walked into our company holiday party completely terrified. How in hell was I going to exist at this boozy party without drinking booze? What was I going to do with my hands without having a drink in my hand? Who was I going to talk to, and were they all going to ask me WHY I didn't have a boozy drink in my hand? I was so flustered I froze.

My secretary saw what was happening, came over, and led me to her table. I don't know what I would have done without her intervention, because she literally saved me that night. I was so insecure about not drinking, not to mention sitting with my secretary instead of sucking up all the free-flowing alcohol with the big muckety-mucks. I actually ended up having an awesome booze-free time thanks to her.

All of which is to say, it's okay if you need someone to hold your hand when you first stop drinking. We're social creatures. You don't have to do this alone.

Eventually, though, I think you'll be surprised at how natural being a non-drinker becomes. A few years after that first booze-free holiday party, I found myself at a conference with a new business partner. I was drinking water during a break, and he looked at my glass and commented, "So you don't drink AT ALL?" I'd told him before I was AF, but I guess he didn't realize I meant always, period, end of story. When I reiterated the "at all" part, he seemed flabbergasted. I, on the other hand, was unperturbed. I wasn't terrified or mortified. I wasn't worried about what he thought. I just didn't care. I don't drink alcohol. It's a fact, plain and simple.

More recently, I was having a lovely lunch outside on a sunny ski day with my husband at Bachelor Gulch in Colorado. People were drinking all around me, and it never even occurred to me that would be a thing to do. I didn't miss alcohol for a second, or even consider it. It was completely irrelevant. A non-issue. I was too busy having a ball listening to music with the man I adore.

This is how life changes as you get years of sobriety under your belt. This is what you have to look forward to. Until then, though, you'll need to learn how to avoid freezing like I did at that company Christmas party or worse, making a bad decision and relapsing because you didn't know what else to do.

As Ben Franklin once famously said, "If you fail to plan, you are planning to fail." That's why I created this handy dandy guide to sticky situations you might find yourself in. It shows you how to politely, humorously, sassily, or even not-so-politely decline the drinks that will still undoubtedly still be offered to you wherever you go.

## Sticky Situation #1: Someone Asks, "Do You Want a Drink?"

When you're first sober, this can seem like the hardest question on SATs. It feels like there aren't even multiple-choice options to use as a guess. Creating an answer on the fly seems damn near impossible.

I don't want you to get caught in that trap, so here are some ways you can answer:

- Say no. Period. That's it. Believe it or not, no is a full sentence.
- If that feels too abrupt or rude to you, try "No, thanks" or "Not right now."
- Order yourself a non-alcoholic drink right away—a sparkling water with lime, iced tea with a lemon, or a Virgin Mary with all the doodads in it. Now you'll have a special drink too and won't feel like everyone is giving you the side-eye.
- Turn the question around and offer to get the drinks for everyone else instead. Ask, "What would YOU like?"
- Befriend the bartender and enlist their help. I'll often say, "Hey, I'm sober. Can you help me not drink tonight? Here's what I'd like every time I need a refill." That way, they're going to be keeping an eye out for me. (I give them a big tip in advance as added motivation.)
- Bring your drink of choice with you. Way back when, I used to bring my own booze supply to parties. Now I bring sparkling water so that I'm sure there will be something available to drink that makes me happy. The beverage itself changed, but the principle stays the same.
- Use humor. Say something like, "I'm going to eat my calories tonight. "

Pick any two of these at a time and try them. Don't try to remember five—you're more likely to freak out and forget them. Having two of these stock phrases preprogrammed in your brain means you'll always have an easy answer at your disposal and avoid any deer-in-the-headlights moments.

## Sticky Situation #2: Someone asks, "WHY aren't you drinking?"

The possibility of being asked this routinely haunts people who are newly sober. They worry: *What are people going to think when I don't order a drink? What am I supposed to tell them?*

First of all, I want you to know that it's pretty unlikely someone would question your choice of beverages. Why would they care? What you put in your glass isn't anybody else's business. If it's any comfort, I've only been asked why I'm not drinking alcohol maybe three times in the twenty-plus years I've been AF.

Second, it's so odd to me that alcohol is a drug you have to justify NOT taking. If somebody weren't a coffee drinker, you wouldn't be trying to shove an espresso down their gullet, right? You don't ask someone, "Why didn't you work out today?" So there's no reason for anyone to force the issue here.

Still, there are some people—and typically they are the ones who have a drinking issue themselves—who will ask, "Hey, what's up with THAT?" They're used to you being their drinking buddy and all of a sudden, you're not drinking. In that case, you have to remember it's actually more about them than it is you, and you're not obligated to answer.

Think of it this way: George W. Bush had a substance abuse problem when he was young, so he doesn't drink anymore. No one elaborates on that, like, *oh, he went to rehab, and now he goes to meetings every day or every week, and he has a sponsor he calls when he is craving a tequila* or whatever. We don't have any idea how he got sober or stays sober. He doesn't owe anyone any explanation, and neither do you.

If you WANT to disclose the reason you're AF, that's an entirely different story. In that case, I generally say I had a problem with alcohol when I was younger, so I don't drink now. Feel free to steal that explanation. Even if you've only been sober a day, you were technically younger yesterday, so it still applies.

Otherwise, here are some responses to have at your disposal. They cover a range of emotions. Whatever mood you're in that night—funny, serious, snarky—pick the one you're feeling and use it.

- "Excuse me, WHAT did you say?" (said in the manner of someone who's just been thrown up on)
- "Why do you ask?"
- "Wow. That's such an interesting question."
- "I'm taking a break."
- "I'm alcohol-free/AF tonight."
- "I don't feel like it."
- "Not right now."
- "When I drink, my clothes fall off." (Frankly, this is my favorite.)

Pick at least three from this list and keep them in mind whenever you go somewhere there will be alcohol—which in our society is pretty much everywhere. That way, you'll always have a snappy answer to people asking something that is none of their business in the first place.

## Sticky Situation #3: You Want to Drink/Crave a Drink

It happens: Despite all your hard work on changing your relationship with alcohol, five o'clock on Thursday night rolls around and you find yourself missing that big ol' glass (or bottle or two) of wine. You're driving past what used to be your favorite bar and you have a sudden craving to turn into the parking lot. You get in a fight with your ex and a bottle of tequila starts sounding like a good listener.

Whenever you're feeling unsure and out of your comfort zone as a newly AF person, I'm going to suggest you substitute one of the five M's or an S for a drink. These are proven ways to get a hit of "happy hormones" and neurotransmitters that don't involve alcohol. And believe it or not, they will actually make you feel better than drinking ever did in the long run. Promise.

- **Masticate.** You know—eat. Preferably sugar. Alcohol has a high sugar content, and it's especially tough to lose alcohol and the sugar all at once. One thing at a time. I used to love sweet drinks (especially champagne) so when I first got sober, I'd keep a Snickers bar in my purse, backpack, and locker at the gym. Yes, I know sugar sucks for you, which is just another reason I don't eat it anymore, but it really helps in getting past that craving phase. Besides, no one has ever gone to jail for eating too much Ben and Jerry's. Please note: sugar fixes stopped working for me after the first months without drinking. Now the pain my body delivers the next day is not worth the short-lived bliss of chocolate. However, at the beginning, sugar was AWESOME.
- **Meditate.** There are so many apps out there—like Calm and Headspace—that teach meditation techniques. Many community centers and yoga studios offer meditation classes. Try some of the available options to see what works best for you. One of my favorite ways to meditate is by using the box breathing method: Breathe in for four counts, hold for four, exhale for four, hold for four. Rinse and repeat for as long as necessary. When you calm your mind and body through meditation, I've found the desire for alcohol generally passes very quickly.
- **Move.** Moving your muscles is another way to get your mind

off drinking. Run as fast as you can. Lift something heavy. Twist yourself into some new yoga contortions. Do anything active. Sweating it out means you're producing endorphins, which means your brain will get a happy hit minus the margaritas.

- **Masturbate.** I mean...if that doesn't make you feel good, you're REALLY in a bad mood. Having an orgasm releases all sorts of pleasurable chemicals in your body. Bonus: It has longer lasting positive effects than that drink you were just obsessing over and will probably make you forget you were ever thinking about it in the first place. My bet is you'll just take a nap instead.

- **Medicate.** There's a drug called naltrexone that may be helpful in decreasing cravings for alcohol. Call your doctor and have the conversation. If nothing else, it's worth trying to see if it helps.

- **Serve.** Research shows that helping someone else lights up the same dopamine pathways as alcohol and drugs. I've washed tons of dishes in sobriety. Whenever I'm uncomfortable in a social situation, I pitch in and help. Don't ask—see where there's a need, step in, and take action. Be of service!

## Sticky Situation #4: Your Family is Driving You Crazy

Spiritual leader Ram Dass once said, "If you think you're enlightened, spend a week with your family." I love that quote. It's just so fucking true.

Being with your family of origin can be incredibly stressful. All the undercurrents and old patterns tend to start bubbling up to the surface. Before long, you're pissing each other off just by breathing the wrong way. And whether or not your other family members are drinking, that intensity can stir up your desire to fall back into your old patterns.

So once again, you need to set yourself up to succeed by making plans. I have a friend who always brings her dog to family events, and her dog just needs so many walks it's ridiculous. Not really, you know, but who's going to argue with her and say the dog doesn't need a walk? I have another friend who also has dogs and will excuse herself early from familial obligations because she has to go take care of her dogs. You can't argue with that either. Now you know why they call dogs (wo)man's best friend.

Other ideas: bring a friend with you on the visit. Don't stay with your mom or whoever triggers you. Limit the amount of time you spend with the fam. Plan activities—watch movies, do some baking, go shopping, play board games, make something together—in an effort to avoid the dreaded conversations. Don't just sit around and talk.

If all that fails, here are some stock phrases to have handy when things get tense and weird:

- "Can we talk later? I want to hear what you have to say but it's too much for me right now."
- "I'm feeling defensive, and I need to take a break."
- "I need to take a nap" or "I need to go to bed."
- "I'm going to go take a drive."
- And don't forget, "I need to go walk the dog." (Even if you don't have a dog.)

## Sticky Situation #5: You're MAD

Some people drink AT a situation or a person. They pour themselves glass after glass, seething the whole time. If you drink when you're pissed, how are you going to handle anger without alcohol?

The first thing to do is to get yourself regulated. Pause, count, take a break, work out, cry, scream. Whatever works.

Next realize that we always—at least in some part—create the situations we're so pissed off about. This is actually great news even though it feels like shit, because if the whole problem lives in the other person, you're completely fucked. The fact is, you can't control anyone but yourself. By admitting you're complicit in some way, you can actually change what you do in the future. The outcome can be different next time.

If you think it's all the other person's fault, you're sadly mistaken. Even if it's as small as your interpretation of what they mean or why they're doing something, we can't ever know what somebody else has in their head. We only THINK we know.

So figure out what you're really mad—or more likely, hurt—about. Then forgive the other person, forgive yourself (for being human), and move on. More on all this in the second half of the book!

## Sticky Situation #6: You're BORED

When you're newly sober, time seems to stretch out in front of you endlessly. It's like, *I'm not drunk. I'm not hungover and sleeping till noon. I don't lose twenty-four of every forty-eight hours anymore. I now have this vacuum of time—what the hell am I supposed to do with it?*

The trick is to find out what you like and pursue that with all your new Juicy AF energy. If you don't know what your "thing" is yet, that's okay. Just keep trying whatever piques your interest. You'll know when you find the right fit.

One client of mine had zero clue what she enjoyed anymore when she quit drinking. Did she like classical music? She had no idea. Hot air ballooning? Not a clue. Building websites? Maybe, maybe not.

She went on a quest to learn what she enjoyed most and was very deliberate about it. She decided to do every single thing that occurred to her, was suggested to her, or she noticed on social media. Now she tells me, "Well, I tried bungee jumping and it sucked. Never doing that again. But I loved surfing. Totally doing that again!"

When Scott Strode first stopped drinking, he saw a brochure with a picture of an ice climber on it and said to himself, "Cool! I want to experience that." Why anyone would choose to climb ice is beyond me, but his take is that it turned out to be a great antidote to boredom because it forces you to stay in the present moment— hearing the crunch of your crampons on the snow and seeing your breath float away is like a meditation. Scott soon learned that physical activity was the most effective tool in his recovery tool kit, and he went on to compete in Ironman races.

Eventually, he even started an organization called The Phoenix, a free sober active community, to help others use physical activity to get and stay sober. The Phoenix doesn't have any of the hurdles a lot of recovery organizations do. You don't have to say you're an alcoholic. All you have to do is sign a waiver that says you haven't used alcohol or drugs in the past forty-eight hours.

Members at The Phoenix get together and do yoga, cycling, CrossFit, hiking, skiing, running, kickball, all kinds of cool activities. It's so safe, it's genius! Everyone is Juicy AF, so there's no worrying about that awkward moment where you're going to have to reveal to a new friend or potential partner that you don't drink.

Personally, my path to eliminating that boredom and vast time vacuum has come through becoming an entrepreneur—very successfully, four times over. I am the shittiest employee. I do not like following rules. I do not like people telling me what to do. I always think I have better ideas. (Proof: My daughter gifted me Post-it Notes® that say, *I'm not bossy, I just have better ideas.*) Now I put my time and creativity into creating companies. It's challenging. It's thrilling. And it is a great way to utilize all that time and energy drinking used to consume in my life.

I've seen people in early sobriety get really upset because they don't know who they are anymore. They take it as this serious, heavy thing, but it's not. Now that you're not weighed down by the anchor of being blasted or trying to recover from being hungover, you're free. Savor that freedom and turn it into FUN.

So forget boredom. We all have an insane amount of creative power. What do you want to create in your Juicy AF life?

## You Are Here. So Where's THERE?

I'm sure you're hoping not drinking isn't always going to be as hard or awkward or painful as it is in the beginning. I mean, it better not be—or quitting isn't fucking worth it, right? I totally get it.

If that's where you're at right now, I have some great news: Your life is going to be miles, worlds, even universes better as a non-drinker. I can promise that if you stick with this (and stick with me here), you will be rewarded with the kind of existence you couldn't even dream of when you were still drinking.

Part Two of this book has been focused on tactical, practical tips and tricks that are enough to help you stop drinking temporarily. On their own, however, they're not what it takes to transform your life into a more satisfying, gratifying, and exciting existence. So don't sell yourself short and stop here—keep going on to Part Three, where you'll learn how to dream your Juicy AF life into reality!

---

## BREAKOUT EXERCISE:
## UNEARTHING YOUR TRUE EMOTIONS

*Seething again? Look below the surface. There's always a deeper feeling hiding underneath anger.*

*The question is, what? Is it sadness? Loss? Grief? Hurt? Identifying the underlying emotion helps you soften into yourself and start letting go of the pain.*

*If you still don't know, try counting your breaths up to ten. Every time you get to ten, ask yourself, what's underneath that? And what's underneath that? And what's underneath that? How did I get hurt? Keep going until you get to the root of it.*

*Next, dig down even deeper. Ask yourself: How did I contribute to the situation? What red flags did I ignore? What needs did I not speak up about? Where wasn't I assertive enough? Where did I make assumptions? Did I pretend to be someone I'm not?*

*Usually, our problem with someone else—our anger—is related to something we don't like or accept about ourselves. Jung called this our shadow, a part of our personality hidden in the unconscious that our conscious mind doesn't recognize as part of our identity. We see another person through that filter and then ascribe that unwanted piece of us to them. Why? Because it's easier to take the stuff we're mad about and project that like a movie on top of another human being than recognize it in ourselves.*

*So find out what's really going on. Accept that reality. Forgive yourself, anyone else involved, and the world. Then, move forward knowing the truth.*

---

# PART THREE

# Create Your Future

Reclaim Your Spirit

# CHAPTER FOUR

# But First, Kay's Spiritual Journey

Everything we've talked about so far has been focused on the short-term—down and dirty fixes that will help get you through those first few months of not drinking. Consider it your immediate triage plan.

But simply removing the booze isn't enough for most of us. I did not go alcohol-free to be miserable. Or small. Or overly serious.

Unless I could create a rich, stimulating, engaging AF life, I would not stay sober. After all, I started drinking for color, excitement, and fun. In order to stay alcohol-free, I needed a healthier, longer-lasting reality with that same color, excitement, and fun. Along the way, I discovered the deeper joy of true connection, being in nature, and expressing myself.

So now, it's time to focus on building a long-term plan for your joyful, interesting, and vital future. This is where your power gets unleashed. Holy crap, the possibilities of what comes next are amazing!

In this section, you'll learn all the best tips, tricks, hacks, and angles to experiment with when reimagining—and then going out and living—your new Juicy AF life. All I ask is that you try what I'm suggesting. Think of it as doing a series of experiments. Some won't land with you, and ideally some will. If a particular experiment or technique isn't working for you, adapt it so it does or move on to the next.

It's time to find out what lights you up. Sparks the most curiosity and excitement in you. What your real purpose on earth is. No, seriously, this is that big and that important.

More than anything, I want you to know that YOU CAN MAKE YOUR LIFE ANYTHING YOU WANT. There are no rules. There is no way to do this "wrong." Everything is up for grabs—so reach for the stars.

## Escaping the Fishbowl

Until now, we've outlined very practical ways to not pick up the first drink. But this is insufficient for living a satisfying and engaging alcohol-free life. After we cut the line to the anchor of alcohol, the question is how are we going to deal with the underlying things that made the oblivion of being drunk so appealing and integral?

Imagine this.

There's a circle—that's our ego.

That circle exists inside a larger circle—our Soul.

And our Soul (or Self with a capital S) is interwoven within a field of divine energy.

There's a protective shell around our ego. That shell is like a fishbowl over our heads. Yes, we can see through it—the trees and chairs and trains are there—and superimposed on top is the image of ourselves reflected back to us. We look at the tree, and we mostly see our likes and dislikes. Our opinions (that girl should *not* be wearing Lycra). Our memories (I remember climbing a tree like that...). Our fears (his indifference means I'm not sexy enough).

The more energy we feed into those images, the denser they get. And that makes it impossible to simply BE with the tree. The chairs. The train.

Our drinking starts inside that fishbowl. The intensity of those projections becomes way the hell too hard to take, and we need relief.

As Steven Pressfield points out in his book *The War of Art*, "Have you ever wondered why the slang terms for intoxication are so demolition-oriented? Stoned, smashed, hammered. It's because they're talking about the Ego. It's the Ego that gets blasted, waxed, plastered. We demolish the Ego to get to the Self."

Shifting the seat of our consciousness is the essential issue at stake.

The view from within the fishbowl is spinny, harshly self-critical, overwhelming.

If getting annihilated on booze or drugs is no longer an option, how do we shift to the seat of the soul?

That's what these next chapters are about.

There are actionable ways to coax your consciousness into shifting. Each suggested practice or experiment is like a peck from a chick's bill fighting its way out from the shell of your ego.

## Following the Spiritual Laws of the Universe

As psychologist Carl Jung once wrote, "Spiritus contra spiritum." The literal translation of that is "spirit against spirit." In other words, the best way to fight addiction is through spirituality—which is why I'm about to teach you the Spiritual Laws of the Universe. When I act in accordance with these Spiritual Laws, my life goes more smoothly.

I used to believe the story I told myself about how I deserved a glass of wine to "take the edge off" (which, of course, led to drinking more than a glass). Using the Spiritual Laws, I've been able to walk through my days without ever developing that edge in the first place. My internal state became less squirrely and itchy when I applied them to my interactions with the world. And the more comfortable I felt in my own skin, the less I needed the "aaaaahhhhh" that came with the first sip of wine.

The Spiritual Laws will act as your guide in creating and living your dream Juicy AF life. They are your homebase, shining light, and facts of life from here on out. You cannot go wrong when you follow them, lean on them, and act in accordance with them. Knowing and working WITH these Spiritual Laws will transform you into a person for whom drinking is irrelevant.

Being human, I sometimes forget to apply the Spiritual Laws. As a fellow human, you probably will, too. Don't beat yourself up over it. Forgive yourself, double down, and try again.

I believe there's a spiritual solution to every problem we encounter. We can all retrain our minds and notice the good, the holy, and the beautiful versus a litany of problems. It's time to find something more positive to concentrate on.

## What Do You Mean, Spiritual?

Let's dig in by defining what "spiritual" means in this context.

I know the word might feel like a turn-off for people who are not into organized religion or were forced into a particular church's way of thought and behavior as a child. So first things first: I'm not using the word spiritual as a synonym for "religious" here, nor am I talking about any specific type of religion or church. Whatever means you use to connect with Nature/God/Love/Universe—or not—doesn't make a difference.

What I'm referring to is our spirit, that which makes up our very essence. Call it a soul. The Divine. Your Higher Self. A wiser, kinder part of you that can observe your thinking and your emotions and reflect on those thoughts and emotions. The words you use don't matter; only the connection you encourage with your spirit does.

Spirituality is a matter of seeing things differently. **And spiritual transformation is the willingness to abide where you are, differently.**

The person I WAS drank. If I didn't change the way I saw and experienced the world, I was going to keep on thinking that first drink was a great idea.

Over the course of my life, I've taken quite a spiritual journey. I grew up in a very religious Christian Dutch Reformed home where we went to church every Sunday (and sometimes also on Wednesdays, and if there was a special event, then maybe on Saturdays, too.) Try as I might, I never connected with any of it. I WANTED to. Sadly, I didn't.

My parents were both teachers, which meant we had a lot of time in the summer but not a lot of money. And so, from the beginning of June through the end of every August, all five of us—my mom, dad, two older sisters, and me—went camping, sleeping in a big blue canvas tent. Most days, my dad was like dawn patrol, out there banging pots and pans. *Rise and shine!* We were expected to get up, eat, and then head out on an all-day hike, during which we'd stop only to identify flowers and birds and maybe grab some lunch.

The rare moments when we weren't doing anything at all were always my favorite. I remember sitting in a meadow singing one day when I was twelve or so. Instantly, I felt a channel to something beautiful, so unknown yet so familiar, open up. I didn't know what it was, but I knew it was something far bigger than myself—yet somehow was also contained WITHIN myself. My heart was so open. I felt connected to everything around me, like the seam between where I ended and where the beauty around me began disappeared. That wholeness, joy, and peace was a profound experience of being spiritually connected. I truly felt myself as a channel for some loving, beautiful energy flowing through me and out into the world.

The way singing made me feel that connection is probably also why I loved being a musician so much. When I played music, everything felt so lined up. I loved that feeling so much I majored in cello in college and eventually became a professional musician. (A VERY practical major, I might add. Hahaha.)

Once I stopped playing, I went looking for something else to fill the spiritual void. I ended up becoming an executive coach and learning how to meditate. I got so into meditation, I even joined a Zen temple. I loved the channel it created and the discipline of it. (I also thought I loved the Zen priest, who decided he was going to divorce his wife so we could get married. I do not miss Drunk Me at all.)

I've always known things without knowing how I know them. There's no rational, literal explanation for how I know. I simply do. For example, when I was a young kid, the phone rang, and I knew immediately that my dad's father had died. I announced to one of my sisters, "Grandpa died." She shot back at me, "That's not a nice thing to say!" And while I can kind of understand where she was coming from, I was right. Now I realize my clairvoyance gets clearer during meditation.

In the first company I started, I leaned very heavily into my clairvoyance, but I still didn't know how to manage it very well. I would sit in meetings and know exactly what everyone was thinking and feeling. I knew what I had to say and do to reel in that one person who wasn't buying what I was selling. I would say to clients, "I know what your big idea is. I can feel it in my body, but I can't access it until I sleep. So, I'll tell you what it is tomorrow." The first time I'd say that they'd all look at me like I was completely unhinged. But by the second time they'd all be like, "Sounds great. Can't wait to hear your ideas in the morning."

My kids have always called me a "psychic satellite." Once my oldest daughter was trying to decide what study abroad program to do. One involved touring the holy sites in northern India. I'd think about that and feel fine. Another option she was considering was in Nepal. I'd think about that one and literally feel like I was being stabbed in the heart.

At first, I was like, *it's just gas*! But every single time I'd think about it, I'd get the same feeling. Not gas, I decided. So I took my daughter to lunch and told her, "Hey, when I think about you in India, I feel great. But when I think about you in Kathmandu, I get a shooting pain in my heart."

Based on that conversation, she decided to go to India but pursued a Tibetan studies program afterwards instead of signing up for Nepal. (She even got to meet His Holiness the Dalai Lama!) And wouldn't you know it, on the exact day she would have landed in Kathmandu, the king declared a state of emergency because of rebel unrest. Nepal got completely cut off from the rest of the world— no travel, no communications, no nothing. (To this day, my family always comes to me and says, "I'm thinking about going to this place. How's your heart? Anything stabbing?")

When one of my girlfriends mentioned going to clairvoyant class a few years back, I was like, *Wait a minute. I want to go, too!* I tried an introductory class, absolutely loved it, and have been going there ever since. (BTW, everyone is clairvoyant. We all have the same channel that I do, but it gets clogged up when we stop trusting our intuition. The practice is in cleaning out that channel and trusting yourself to get it working again. I'll introduce you to some of the visualization practices I learned to help unclog that channel in upcoming chapters.)

I eventually became an ordained minister through that school. I now use the psychic skills I've honed there to help people during pivotal, transitional moments in their lives—like quitting drinking. I've found that connection I was always looking for through a metaphysical lens.

Today, I tap into the Universe through the Spiritual Laws I'm going to share with you in the next chapters. It's like having access to a wiser, more experienced, more confident partner—except that it's part of my consciousness. What a great way to stay on track!

Acting in accordance with these Spiritual Laws aligned my thoughts and my actions, bringing me freedom from shame, clearmindedness about who I am, and being happy with myself. It's amazing. All the external signs of this happiness with myself—the great marriage, the loving family, the career success—are simply that: external symptoms and ramifications of my internal sense of liking myself. Imagine that!

Of course, I forget and struggle sometimes. We all do. No shame there. When that happens, I simply refocus and keep going.

Even though the Spiritual Laws are invisible, that doesn't mean they aren't constantly at play. Have you ever seen gravity? No, of course not. But you CAN see its effects. The same is true for these Spiritual Laws. Their effects happen inside us first, then reverberate throughout our lives into our relationships, our health, and our success.

I want you to feel that same self-love, reverberation, and connection. Have that same trust in yourself. To know that the Universe cooperates when your intention is to extend love: the good, the holy, the beautiful.

All that comes through the Spiritual Laws and applying them to your life, so let's get started.

# CHAPTER FIVE

# Spiritual Law #1

## WHAT YOU THINK ON GROWS

**Your goal for this chapter: Visualize your dream Juicy AF life—and then start to live it NOW.**

Buddha declared, "We are shaped by our thoughts; we become what we think." In *Hamlet,* Shakespeare wrote, "There is nothing either good or bad but thinking makes it so." Oprah's version is, "You become what you believe."

I used to sit around at night cataloging everything I did wrong during that day. I'd come up with the perfect retort ten hours too late. Or I'd think, *oh my God, I must have looked or sounded like such an idiot!*

I've since learned how to focus on what I want to grow instead: amusement, gratitude, a sense of fun, and good health. It can be hard to rid ourselves of useless, negative thoughts, but it is well worth the effort. I now know how to celebrate my wins and I'm not using those experiences I formerly thought of as "losses" as data points that prove what a piece of shit I am anymore. Today, I learn from my challenges so I can do better in the future.

The program with "those" meetings suggests a daily practice of taking an inventory of where during the day you were selfish, resentful, dishonest, and afraid. While this might work well for guys who have insufferably bloated egos, it is self-defeating for women like me whose fundamental fear is of our inadequacy. That practice is not an antidote to the story "I'm not enough"; in fact, it deepens it.

So I created a different practice.

At the end of the day, I write down what I did well. If things didn't go the way I'd hoped, I come up with a list of things I could do differently next time. That way, I have a plan for when I encounter a similar situation. I focus on my growth, progress, and successes. Any mistakes I make become fuel for more growth.

I believe in the power of visualization. No, not the kind where you sit around doing nothing at all and expect bags of money and a mansion and your dream partner to be delivered to your door. I'm talking about actively envisioning what and who you want to become—and then acting like she's already here. This can literally work miracles in your life.

Here's a look at the power of visualization in action. Example one: Edmund Jacobson, a Harvard physiologist, did a study on muscle growth. In it, he had people imagine lifting an object. They literally only THOUGHT about it. What he found was this simple act of envisioning this happening effectively triggered electrical activity in the muscles that would have been involved in doing the actual exercise. Crazy, right?

Example two: researcher Guang Ye questioned Jacobson's results, so he designed another study, this one focusing on strengthening finger muscles (why finger muscles? we don't know). In it, he assigned participants to one of three groups. The first group did nothing at all, the second practiced finger exercises, and the third visualized those same exercises but didn't actually do them. At the end of the study, the first group unsurprisingly reported no increase in finger strength. Also unsurprising was that the group that exercised saw finger strength increase by 53 percent. What might be surprising, though, was that the group that only THOUGHT about doing the exercises also showed a significant strength increase—35 percent, in fact. (Now imagine how big those increases would have been if participants practiced visualization AND did the exercises!)

Example three: Natan Sharansky was a chess prodigy imprisoned in Russia. To help endure his time in prison, he visualized playing chess master Garry Kasparov every day, and in every mental game he won. When Natan was finally released, he got the chance to actually play Kasparov—and won! All because he trained his mind to win against Kasparov, whether that was in his imagination or IRL.

That's how much power our minds have to create new realities! We can think our way to becoming stronger, better, and more successful. Or we can do the opposite. Which do you want to choose?

## Envisioning a New You

Now that you know visualization is a key way to transform, it's time to start envisioning the new Juicy AF you. A woman I sponsor saw a picture of her drinking self versus her sober self in her mind's eye. Her drinking self—and I'm quoting her here—looked like "a fat old lady wearing a flannel shirt holding a beer in one hand and a TV remote in the other." Her sober self, on the other hand, was an attractive, smiling, relaxed woman wearing flowing white garments and doing yoga on a gorgeous Caribbean beach. The stark contrast between the two is what motivated her to become the Juicy AF woman in her vision.

Not sure where to start? Don't worry, I've got you. We're going to discuss a variety of ways to envision exactly what you want your Juicy AF life to become.

Write down everything that occurs to you as you work through the exercises in this section. Don't second-guess yourself or self-edit. Trust that you know what you desire and who you truly are deep down inside. If you see it, say it.

I want you to treat this as sacred work because it is. Get a special notebook. Bonus points if it has a picture on it that symbolizes creativity and rebirth. Buy yourself some special pens while you're at it. I use turquoise and bright pink glitter gel pens—they make me happy. They probably won't work for endorsing a check, but who cares? Besides, I use Venmo anyway.

Put your special journal and special pens in a special place where they will stay private. This is just for you, and you don't have to show anyone what you're working on. When you go back to reread what you've written later, I think you'll be amazed.

## EXPERIMENT #1: ENVISION YOUR EULOGY

The whole premise of this exercise is to begin with the end in mind (props to Stephen Covey's *Seven Habits of Highly Successful People* for introducing this concept). As macabre as this might sound, I want you to imagine what you're going to be eulogized for at your funeral or memorial service. What do you want to be remembered for? What do you want people to say about you? How do you want to have shown up in their world?

David Brooks, author of *The Road to Character,* talks about résumé virtues and eulogy virtues. Résumé virtues can be summed up in words like problem-solver, team player, and self-starter. Eulogy virtues are qualities like patience or kindness or lightheartedness.

For this exercise, I want you to think about eulogy virtues. Forget the résumé ones. No one will care that you were a "people person" once you're dead, but they will care that you were a kind person who brought dinner to friends who were feeling down, or offered free babysitting to overwhelmed new moms, or always remembered their birthday. Kindness, generosity, compassion, and the actions that express these qualities—those are what leave a lasting impression, even beyond our time on earth.

Another way to start thinking about this is, what attitude do you want to bring to your new Juicy AF life? I had to pay for gas inside the little mini-mart the other day, and the guy in front of me was muttering an angry stream of words. I met the eyes of the woman behind the counter, and she said, "Oh, that's just how Jerry is. He's grumpy, and we love him for it." Underneath all that spewing he may be a nice guy, but I don't want to be known as Grumpy Jerry after I'm gone, do you? No! So make sure your attitude is one you want associated with who you are.

If you're like, *oh, fuck, this is WAY too hard to think about,* I've broken it down into five areas of life to make envisioning your future eulogy easier. What can I say? I'm just giving (one of my eulogy virtues!) like that.

The first area to consider is spirituality. What do you want to experience spiritually in this life? I'm not talking about attending church every Sunday (although if that's your thing, go for it). Like, wouldn't it be cool to achieve enlightenment?

I want you to know that having a spiritual experience can put you into an altered state of mind that's more fun than being plastered could ever be. Things can happen that are way cooler and weirder and farther out than you can begin to imagine. Doesn't that sound worth exploring?

Personally, the spiritual experiences I've had since I got sober have been far more interesting and meaningful than anything that ever happened to me when I was drinking. I went to clairvoyant school. I became an ordained minister. I even took some epic shamanic journeys, like the time I had a kundalini awakening in Qigong class.

The teacher had told us to move our bodies from side to side, arms outstretched but still loose like jelly. So there I was twisting, my arms hitting my back with every turn. And there the teacher was, playing a glass singing bowl, its sound ricocheting around the studio.

After the exercise ended, he asked us to describe what we experienced. Some people said they felt energized. Others were tired—they were the ones sweating profusely. I raised my hand and blurted out, "My body's moving but I'm not the one moving it. What's going on here?"

Apparently, I was having a kundalini awakening. According to the kundalini practice, there are two streams of energy living at the base of our spines. These energy streams are always running up and down our spines, intertwining like a physician's symbol (which is called a caduceus, BTW). When that energy gets activated, it can shoot up and out the top of our heads—which is exactly what happened to me. I literally shook for three days because of all the energy I released during that class.

Just saying, nothing trippy like that ever happened to me when I was drinking—and hell yes, I want to experience things like that. My life is so much fuller having pursued these paths. Today, I'm at a place where my spiritual juju is really activated and I'm loving it.

Family is another domain to consider here, however you choose to define your family. I think of mine as my husband, our three kids, and my mom, plus a few special friends. My family includes people I'm connected to by birth and people I'm connected to by choice.

Who do you consider your family? What do you want your role to have been within that circle of beloved people? How do you want to be remembered by them?

The next one is social, aka play. What experiences do you want to have had by the end of your life? How do you want to have played? Now that you're sober, you can go jump out of an airplane if you want to. You can learn to snowboard. You can join a band. Try a bunch of things and see what sticks. Whatever you do for the sheer joy of it is where you belong. People will remember you for what your passions were.

Next up, there's career and education. What do you want to be known for in those realms? It doesn't have to be, *I earned my PhD*. It could be, *She always treated all our customers with compassion* or *she was so intellectually curious, she took continuing ed classes all the time* or *she knew everything there was to know about kundalini because she once had this wild awakening in Qigong class.* Oh, wait, that last one was about me again, wasn't it?

Finally, think about community. Again, however you want to define that is up to you, but what do you want to do to make a lasting impact on yours? Maybe it's *she couldn't stand the thought of orphans in China, so she created a nonprofit to help them.* Or *she volunteered with her local firefighting brigade.* Or *whenever a new neighbor moved in, she always baked brownies and took them over welcoming them to the neighborhood.*

Your contribution can be on whatever scale you want as long as it is meaningful to you and the people you're serving.

EXPERIMENT #2: HIDE AND SEEK

The second way to start to envision what's possible for your new Juicy AF life is to think about the "before times." And what I mean by that is, before puberty and before you started drinking. What were you drawn to?

I have three kids. When my son was little, he was crazy about cars. He had this little plastic contraption—it was red with a yellow steering wheel and a blue shifter—that fit over his lap and simulated driving. He lived under that thing. He could play with it all day. So it was no surprise to me that in his adult life, his passion project is related to cars. Porsches, to be exact.

One of my daughters was drawn to creative projects. She loved all those little kits for making pom-pom animals, felted wool characters, latch hook rugs, clay figurines, beaded jewelry, Shrinky Dinks, you name it. When she was six or seven, we were both working on a project that had us making angels out of glitter, feathers, pipe cleaners, and googly eyes. She looked over at mine and said, "Oh, mom, that's pathetic. You're not good at this. Let me do it for you." Today, she's an art director for commercials.

My other daughter was super into jigsaw puzzles. She could turn all the pieces over and put them together upside down. She was always trying to talk one of us into coming over and doing the puzzle with her, and whenever we'd get a single piece in place, she'd cheer for us like it was the greatest accomplishment ever. Meanwhile, she'd fit like twenty pieces into the puzzle in the time we struggled to get one. She's studying engineering now.

And then there's me. My second-grade teacher had us write our autobiographies—which is fucking hilarious because we were seven years old at the time—but I loved that assignment. It's one of the few things from my childhood that my mother saved. In it, I wrote that I wanted to be either a secretary (all I could imagine a woman in business being at the time), a missionary who travels the world, or a nurse who is a healer. Well, now I'm a spiritual teacher and I'm helping heal people from alcohol addiction through my new company, Juicy AF.

The point being: we all know who we are. We know what we like. We know what we're good at. We know that when we're three, four, five, six, seven, eight years old. If whatever that is got shamed out of you, or you decided it wasn't valid, or it wouldn't make you enough money to support you or impress enough people—forget all that. Whatever was hidden away, go find it again.

I think by the time we grow up we've been so inundated with social media and family expectations and societal crap that we forget what we love. Kids in college now aren't learning because they're super-curious about the anatomical structure of a leaf or how the novel of *Don Quixote* relates to the tone poem by Richard Wagner—everybody's like, "Oh, is that going to look good on my résumé?" And that sucks.

Sure, we have to conform to society in certain ways. We'd get eaten by the lion on the savanna if we didn't. But at the same time, I think that just deadens us to what we want. This is the path to rediscovering your childlike spirit. This is where the juice is, where your heart and soul lie.

Go looking for that. Let me know what you find.

EXPERIMENT #3: DREAM ON

Another way to start envisioning the life you want to create is by daydreaming, like my client did when she saw her non-drinking self dressed in white on the beach doing yoga. Don't be practical here. As Daniel Burnham, the architect and city planner who designed Chicago and ensured all that gorgeous public lakefront access once said:

> Make no little plans; they have no magic to stir men's blood and probably themselves will not be realized. **Make big plans; aim high in hope and work**, remembering that a noble, logical diagram once recorded will never die, but long after we are gone will be a living thing, asserting itself with ever-growing insistency.

Imagine where you're waking up in your shiny new life. Who is next to you? What do you see out your window? When you look in the mirror, what does your hair look like? What kind of clothes are you wearing? What are you eating for breakfast? Get as specific about it as possible.

Maybe you'll say, "I want to wake up and see a pasture and my horse frolicking." Or, "I want to look out my window and see the Eiffel Tower (or the ocean, or Madison Avenue, or the Nile)". Maybe you'll see a color. Maybe you'll hear something. Maybe something will just come to you, and you won't have a clue how you know it, but you do.

If an image pops into your head, believe it. Trust yourself here. There's plenty of time to second-guess it later.

Whatever you do, don't believe the bullshit narrative in your ingrained thinking: *Oh, that'll never happen. I don't deserve that. That's crazy, or at the very least unrealistic.* You don't need to know how you're going to get there. Just write it down. If you see it, say it, right?

Remember that strategic plan I developed for my thirty-ninth year? Where I wrote that I wanted to drink less? And said I'd go to one of "those" meetings if all my other ideas to make myself stop drinking so much failed? Well, I put that plan away in a drawer and totally forgot about it the second my pen left the paper.

Yet I did end up going to a meeting—on the day before I turned forty—without even remembering I'd made that deal with myself 364 days earlier. In fact, I didn't even realize until I was two years sober. When I cleaned out that drawer and found what I'd written, I was absolutely floored.

The magic was in the intention. I knew what I wanted, and so do you—even if that's buried somewhere deep down inside you. Let that out. Write it down. Make it happen.

EXPERIMENT #4: VISION QUEST

I made a vision board when we moved to Colorado—and absolutely every last little thing on it has come true. Lest you think it was all spiritual, hippy-dippy, do-unto-others kind of aspirations, let me assure you I pasted a picture of a diamond ring I coveted onto it.

Also pictured was a woman meditating with a glorious beam of light coming out of her head. Another was snowshoeing. Still others were horseback riding, hiking, and scuba diving.

There were photos of small, local, natural food brands. There was a house surrounded by a forest with floor to ceiling windows. There were romantic couples looking like they were head over heels in love. And of course, that big honking diamond ring.

I drew lines between all the pictures in different colors on that board. I wrote down my eulogy values: gratitude, humility, amusement. And then I rolled it up and stuck it in a closet.

But behold, again like magic, today I live in a house surrounded by forest with floor to ceiling windows. I created (and later sold) a natural food company. I've been diving and hiking and meditating and horseback riding. And my husband gave me that coveted diamond for our twentieth wedding anniversary. When I opened the box, I started laughing, that's how big and beautiful it is.

So now it's your turn. Go buy a big pile of magazines. Cut out whatever picture, headline, word, or image grabs your attention and paste it onto your board. Don't think about it, just do it.

Start inviting your life to become what you always dreamed it could be.

### EXERCISE #5: YOU TELL ME

Dan Sullivan, founder of a coaching program for entrepreneurs called The Strategic Coach Program, developed an exercise in which you ask the people who love you most (or at least like you a lot) to give you feedback about your strengths. The questions they need to answer are:

- What do you value about me?
- What do I bring to our relationship?
- What do you count on me for/what problems do you come to me for help with?
- Where do you see me light up?

Whenever I suggest doing this with the women I mentor, I get a lot of pushback. They typically say something like, "That's gross—it's obligating somebody to say something nice about me." Or, "No way, I'm too embarrassed!" If that's your initial reaction, don't worry—everybody feels that way.

Yeah, but I'm STILL going to challenge you to do it. Having other people recognize your gifts gives you insight into the pieces of yourself you can't see from where you're sitting right now. As the saying goes, you can't read the label from inside the jar.

It's like this: my first-grade teacher, Mrs. Grabinsky, was so much fun. We got gold stars for every book we read that year, so I read more books—by a long shot—than anyone else in class. She was giving me strokes for what I already loved to do! Imagine me writing a letter to her explaining how serious my family was, and how her sense of playfulness and encouragement was exactly what I needed in that moment to feel okay in the world. That would make her feel like an amazing teacher and person (which she was)—and it would also make me feel great to tell her how much she meant to me.

Well, that's what this exercise is, only in reverse. Think of it as a gift you're giving to the people you love, not something embarrassing or icky or like you're begging for compliments. So go on now—write the email, tell your people they have ten days to respond, and push send. (If they don't get back to you, IT DOESN'T MEAN THEY DON'T LOVE YOU. It just means they're busy. That's all.)

When you get your letters back, start looking for the through line. I did this by printing mine out and taking different color highlighters to the words and phrases that kept coming up. One thing I kept getting consistent feedback on was being a fast read of any situation, a nod to my intuition (well, my mom wrote, *you're a fast reader* and I was like, close enough). I can walk into any situation and know exactly what's going on without anyone having to explain it to me. Getting my letters confirmed for me that having a leadership role, creating a spiritual community, using my clairvoyance to heal people, and becoming an entrepreneur—all with a sense of lightheartedness and amusement—is exactly where I'm meant to be.

A note of caution: Our human tendency is to dismiss the things that come easily to us. It's so obvious in our heads that we just assume it's that obvious to everybody else, and therefore we diminish it rather than owning it. We think *oh, everybody does that*. Um, no. Not true.

As I said earlier, I've always known things without knowing how I know them, like when the phone rang, and I instantly knew that my grandpa had died. I used to think everyone did that, but I know now everyone certainly cannot do that.

Or let's look at the opposite kind of example: You never want me in charge of invoicing because I will fuck it up royally. It'll be in such a tangle, it will take nine human beings who are great at finances to untangle it.

And that's the point: Somebody else's greatest gift is often the stuff we suck at and hate to do. And vice versa. The things we're gifted at may seem inconsequential to us because they're so flipping easy, but those are exactly the things we should do more of and offer to more people. That's the value we add to this world.

Strategic Coach' has created a concept and exercise called Unique Ability' that helps eliminate that tendency to downplay our strengths. In it, you put all the things you do over the course of a day or a week or month or a year into one of four columns: Incompetent, Competent, Excellent, and Unique Ability'. Your job is then to focus on the things you're already excellent and unique at.

Fun fact: It takes the same amount of time and energy to go from incompetent to competent as it takes to go from excellence to unique. The problem with going from incompetent to competent is we're only ever going to be competent, which makes us feel shitty about ourselves. But if we invest the same amount of time and energy going from excellent to unique, it makes us hugely more successful and happier in our own skin. Excellent to unique is also a lot more fun and contributes a hell of a lot more to the world.

The point of this whole exercise is to find, acknowledge, and then focus on the things you are excellent and/or unique at. These are our gifts, and they're far more valuable to us than the stuff that we suck at. That's what lights us up, and what lights us up is our gift to the world.

Imagine ignoring what the world needs from us so we get better at, say, bookkeeping. (Oh, wait, that's me again, isn't it?)

## The Big Hope

Once you've completed all these exercises (using your special journal and your special pens), reread what you've written from each angle of inquiry and look for three to seven recurring themes. Make sure at least a handful of them are eulogy qualities or attitudes like funny or insightful or helpful. Put an equal focus on HOW you're going to show up in your new Juicy AF life as WHAT you're going to do and WHERE you're going to do it.

These themes are now your clues to finding your true place in the world. Don't worry about how you're going to get there just yet. Don't put a timeframe on it. Just paint the picture of what that looks like. This is where your big hope for the future lives.

When you are writing about what you've experienced during these experiments, my encouragement is to focus on what you feel great about. Write about what you did well, and you will continue to do those things well. What we focus on grows.

If you missed the mark somewhere, don't worry. That just becomes awesome fodder, more grist for the mill. What did you learn? What are you going to try next time instead? Do not let a painful experience go to waste!

This is not about self-flagellating, though. No hair shirt needed. It's all in the spirit of curiosity.

I think of it this way: my mistakes are the fuel for my growth and ability to help others. And because I continually make mistakes, I have lots of fuel for an exponential amount of growth. When I feel icky about something I did (or didn't do), I rewind the tape (yes, I'm old) and ask myself to create ten different ways I could have seen and responded to the situation. What spiritual principle could

I have embodied? And then I write about how I will apply my best ideas the next time I encounter a similar situation.

## Activating Your Subconscious

With your big hope in focus, it's time to engage your subconscious to help you attain it. I believe the subconscious holds far more power than the conscious mind. When the subconscious gets involved, things begin to unfold in ways we can't even imagine.

Lately I've been envisioning myself wearing a bright pink out-fit on the Macky Auditorium stage at the University of Colorado Boulder. My husband is standing in the wings. Two thousand Juicy AF women are in the audience, and I say something that makes me laugh. The audience cracks up with me. Then I just double over with laughter, a case of the giggles and absolute euphoria overtaking me because my dream is coming true.

I can see this in my mind's eye, plain as day. I have faith that my subconscious is already at work to put it in motion. I know it is going to come true. I think what's going to crack me up the most when it actually happens is, *oh my God, this is exactly how I imagined it!*

Activating your subconscious can work wonders in your life, but here's the tricky part: Your subconscious needs to accept the idea you're presenting before it can help bring it into reality. And to do this, we need to tap into the power of our literal minds.

## Imbuing Your Thoughts with a Feeling

Want to know why affirmations don't work? Because if you don't actually believe them, the subconscious calls bullshit. The message bounces right off our brains.

For example, my predominant emotion in the past was, *I'm not worthy because I'm not good enough.* I felt that so deeply my subconscious was like, *Roger that, let's go make it happen.* It became the lens through which I interpreted all my experiences, and so I kept having more of them. At the time, if I had told myself the opposite message—*you are valuable*—it wouldn't have had enough emotional electrical charge to dislodge my built-in preconceived notions.

To work my way out of that kind of conundrum, I have learned to imbue my thoughts with feeling. To help in that regard, I use all five senses when visualizing. I concentrate on what I might smell, hear, touch, and taste, giving the experience all the dimensions possible to convince my mind of its validity and truth.

Visuals are especially effective here. Envisioning a vignette of yourself in a future scenario, like I did with my speaking gig, is a method that works well. Creating a vision board is another. Yet another is imagining a movie screen in front of you—the red drapes part, and you watch a preview of coming attractions that you want to experience in life. Our vision of our future is actually more compelling to our subconscious than anything to do with our past, so make it as vibrant as you possibly can.

Visuals allow your subconscious to accept an idea even if you don't quite believe it yourself yet. This is how to MAKE yourself believe it. It works because you're an observer of things happening to you, watching yourself succeed like you would an adored child.

## It's an Inside Out Job (Not Outside In)

I was an unhappy cog in the wheel at a global organization when I was still drinking. I kept trying to arrange my OUTSIDE world to make myself happy. Once I got sober, I launched my first entrepreneurial venture and learned that my happiness actually comes from INSIDE, when I am in my "lit up" place. I made six times as much money as I ever had before. I traveled the world. I married the love of my life. I adopted a beautiful child. I wrote a book. My entire existence became exponentially bigger and more interesting.

That same kind of energy and creativity explosion is available to every woman who decides to stop the spiral and successfully cut the cord on the alcohol anchor. Once you're clear about your true place in the world and your greatest gifts—the things that totally light you up—you can start working with the Universe to get what you want rather than looking elsewhere for it. The way things come to us when we work within the universal flow is so much more magnificent than anything or anyone else could ever give us, or that we could produce on our own.

## Onward!

So far, you've worked with a variety of tools to get a pulse on your true place in the world. You remembered what you loved doing when you were little. You imagined an alternative life for yourself. You daydreamed and made a vision board. You wrote down everything you want to do and experience in your new Juicy AF life.

Now you can see your ideal future self, your own version of that calm, peaceful lady in white doing yoga on the beach. I want you to know that I can see her, too. She's giving you a thumbs up. And the time to start showing up as her is NOW.

If you're thinking, *but I have no clue how to do that*, never fear. These next chapters show you how to bring your ideal future self into reality. BTW, she's a fucking badass beauty and I can't wait to meet her.

---

## BREAKOUT EXERCISE:
## SELF-LOVE AND POSITIVITY

*Close your eyes and take three deep breaths. Imagine a tail—this can look like an actual tail, a Slip 'N Slide, a hollow peppermint stick, or whatever you want it to—*

reaching from the tip of your tailbone down into the center of the earth. (Middle earth can also look like whatever you want it to look like. It doesn't have to be a fiery ball of molten rock. For me, it looks like a coral reef.) Anything that's not serving you, send down to your tailbone, through your tail, and into the center of the earth. Put some weight on it and leave it there. Whatever negative energy was attached to those thoughts is now transformed into something neutral and stored far away from you.

Next, imagine a giant golden sun at least twice as high and tall as you over the top of your head. Whatever emotion you want to feel—self-love, amusement, forgiveness, joy, whatever—is embodied within it. As soon as that sun is nice and full and round and glowing and sparkly and has just the right color and vibration, pop a hole in the bottom of it and let the beautiful feelings come pouring through the crown of your head. Let them flood your entire system—from your forehead to your sinuses, to your jaw, to your throat, to your shoulders, to your heart, through your abdomen, down your legs, down your arms. Doesn't that feel great? When I do this every morning, I ask myself, what vibe do I want to live in today? Gratitude and amusement are my favorites. What are yours?

Another thought to try here: I like to imagine I have a loving guide who follows me everywhere. Can you see me pointing to her right now? She's a little bit behind me, maybe a foot above my head. She loves me with such tenderness and such a full heart. When I can't quite muster loving feelings as big as hers about myself, I try to look at myself from her perspective.

Or imagine looking at yourself onstage through your own eyes—like you are your own mother or your older, wiser *self. Do you feel a surge of love, compassion, and wanting only the best for yourself? Do you want to comfort yourself and tell yourself everything is okay? What kind words of wisdom does your older, higher self have for you today?*

---

# CHAPTER SIX

# Spiritual Law #2

## SUBSTITUTE NEW BEHAVIORS FOR OLD ONES

Your goal for this chapter: Let go of unproductive old thoughts and behaviors by substituting them with newer, truer ones.

We've already talked about how ineffective willpower is. If you try to eliminate a harmful way of thinking or acting without replacing it with a more helpful thought or action, it leaves a void that will eventually get filled back in by—you guessed it—that same unhelpful thing you tried to get rid of in the first place. As Aristotle said, nature abhors a vacuum!

Escaping an old behavior or idea requires substituting a new one to replace it. You must grow something positive in the place formerly occupied by a negative habit or thought. Substitution is the only effective way I've found to change thoughts and behaviors for the long-term.

What we feed energy and attention to grows exponentially. Let's work on personal transformation from a place of understanding for where we are now, and where we want to go in the future. Let's start substituting new behaviors to get free of old ones.

## F*ck Freud

Since the time of Freud, our culture has believed that there's a straight line from whatever happened to us as children to where we are now. Whatever the story we've told ourselves about it makes our brains go looking for more evidence to support that theory, so we just keep fulfilling that same destiny. Eventually, we even start to believe that story contains our entire identity.

My first boss was an Army guy. Apparently in the military, if they've decided you are a problem for whatever reason, they make a book noting all of the evidence supporting that conclusion. That's called "keeping book" on somebody. That's exactly what we do to ourselves when we start believing our old stories.

Whenever we start thinking negative thoughts about ourselves—like, *That was really dumb. I'm such a loser. I feel like an idiot*—we can barely concentrate on anything else. Our old stories about how flawed we are and what failures we are and what we do wrong are so deeply ingrained that simply telling ourselves, *I'm just not going to think that anymore* doesn't work. And then all we want to do is get numb to get that voice to shut the fuck up.

We're not doing that anymore, right? There's a better way. Here's how.

## Start Digging

As psychiatrist Carl Jung once wrote, "Until you make the unconscious conscious, it will direct your life and you will call it fate." In other words, the ingrained thoughts and stories we've been telling ourselves have been running our lives up until now. To change that, we need to bring those stories to the surface and start telling ourselves new and more empowering ones in their place.

This is where that ability to think critically about our thinking is powerful. We can look at the stories we've hung onto to give meaning to our lives through the eyes of our older, wiser selves and see them for what they truly are: ideas we've invented and clung to that have helped us get to where we are and may no longer be helpful to us.

We're going to start this exercise by unearthing our painful, old stories. We're not doing this to punish ourselves or tell ourselves we're bad people. We're not looking for our flaws or what's defective in us. We're doing it so we can FREE ourselves from whatever got programmed into us when we were born into the families we came into, at this place, and at this time. The goal is to substitute a powerful spiritual antidote for each one of these old stories. Freedom FROM these old stories creates the freedom TO create a juicier, more interesting, and joyful future. This is how we change our "fate."

Here's what those old stories looked like for me: I was born into a family that was very, very, very quiet. We'd have dinner and then everybody would retreat to their rooms to do homework. My parents were both teachers. At night, they graded papers. They didn't have much of a social life. On Friday nights they'd go to the library and read. My dad in particular was such an introvert that I think he would have been diagnosed as being on the spectrum today.

My two older sisters fit perfectly into this family dynamic—and then there was me. I am a huge extrovert. I played the cello. I was a cheerleader. I had the lead in school plays. I needed noise. I needed color. I needed a big social life.

Because I was nothing like the rest of my family, I created the story, *There's really something fucking wrong with me existentially. The way that I am in the world isn't right. I'm not lovable because of how I am. People don't like me the way I am. I have to tamp myself down. I have to be quieter. I shouldn't be so loud and fun.*

Another example: I once worked with a beautiful, bright young woman who walked through life with a giant chip on her shoulder. No matter what a client or one of our bosses or flight attendants said, her immediate response was, "They're trying to screw me over." She took her interpretation of the most innocuous of interactions as evidence to support her thesis. For whatever reason, our brains want to be right.

Old stories make life completely confounding. They make being happy virtually IMPOSSIBLE. Until we unearth our old stories, there's no way to apply the antidote.

Dig down deep.

## Play the Blame Game

Next, I want you to identify the people you blame for all the experiences you've had and where you are now. Maybe that's your ex-husband, your mother, your kids, or your boss. Write down all the names of people who are just fucking wrong—how they hurt you, made you angry, ruined your life.

Now, pick just one of them and list everything they did to you and why they're to blame for it. Keep digging. Go far enough back in your life and your interactions with that person to pinpoint where this all began.

For example, I met my first husband when I was still a teen, and he was thirty-seven. I was a music student, and he played in a world-famous symphony. He was at the pinnacle of his profession, and I was aspiring to achieve what he already had. He traveled the world, drove a Porsche, and most importantly, dated both a Miss Wisconsin and a dancer in the New York City Ballet. I thought if I could get him to pick me over those amazingly beautiful and talented women, that would be my validation that I was actually okay in this world.

Of course, I married him. And then he proceeded to let me know in ten thousand subtle and not-so-subtle ways a day how wrong

I was. It barely fazed me. That message 100 percent matched my internal narrative. It felt completely normal to me by then.

Pretty soon, I felt like I was spinning a hologram out in front of me of what I thought my life should look like to other people. I was Princess fucking Leia with that thing. I assumed everyone lived like that, and literally believed my best friend and her husband were pretending harder than my husband and I were to be happy, and that's why they were happier than we were. (Um, no. That's not how things actually work.)

This new *you're not pretending well enough* narrative—coupled with my *you're not good enough, you're existentially flawed, how you are in this world is wrong* ones—created so much fear and angst in me that being numb was preferable. Drinking became my way to escape that horrendous inner harangue of *not good enough, not thin enough, not sexy enough, not pretty enough, you'll never, ever, EVER be enough.*

And when I wasn't too busy being not enough, it seemed I tended to veer into being way the fuck too much. I always overshot the mark, which didn't leave a lot of wiggle room for being comfortable. Think of a campfire: I was either on the outside of the circle in the cold and dark, or I was in the fucking flame. What I really wanted to be was sitting in the circle, but I had no clue how to get there.

And it was all his fucking fault...or was it?

## Determine Where You Are Complicit

When I first got sober, I was furious with my ex-husband for the way he treated me. Once I dug down deep enough into the muck, though, I realized I made choices to be in that relationship based on really superficial and self-centered reasons. I was like, *oh, that's how I participated. I was complicit. I played a role in this. I encouraged this for my own benefit.* Marrying somebody because of their car, job, and beautiful ex-girlfriends is not nice. Once it became apparent to me, all my anger—well, most of it, anyway—dissolved.

I married my current husband because I love being with him. He's this sensitive spiritual soul in a really masculine body, which is just so intoxicating to me. The way he interacts with our kids is amazing. When they were teens and would do something outrageously stupid, he would make his point by finding a way to make them laugh at themselves. I just find him so magical. I love him for who he is, I think it's such a privilege to be around him, and those things that attracted me to him are still wildly attractive to me. It's not *what can I get out of this situation*, but a completely different orientation.

I have a lot of compassion for my eighteen-year-old self who married for the wrong reasons. Unconsciously, I chose to repeat the story I created about myself as a kid and bring it to my first marriage. That's all I knew. But it also proves my point about how we contribute to our circumstances, which is why reinterpreting your past is so powerful. We are always responsible for our choices and our perceptions.

The first step to changing our stories is taking some responsibility for our circumstances rather than blaming everybody else for everything, which is how most people are when they're drinking: *It's my mother's fault. It's my sister's fault. It's my ex-husband's fault. If only he would have done this or that. They hurt me. It's all their fault, not mine.* Finding fault outside of ourselves only shuts off growth. It keeps us trapped in our old lives.

So ask yourself: In what ways did I somehow help create my experiences through the decisions I made or the attitudes I adopted? What did I have to believe in order to make those choices? What did I want, what was I trying to get out of the situation, what responsibility was I evading, and why was that important to me?

The victim story keeps you trapped in the drinking spiral. It's time to set that story down and create a more powerful idea and choice of yourself.

## Tell Yourself a New Story

Most people with alcohol problems are afraid to take a hard look at themselves because it seems like maybe it's gotten too ugly and wormy and dank and musty in there. It feels like going into the basement to see if there's a dead body down those stairs. So if that's where you're at, I get it—and do it anyhow.

We conjured our old stories to make sense out of our experiences in the world. We clung to them because they somehow served us—we wouldn't still believe them so strongly otherwise. If we had compelling evidence to the contrary, we would have already changed our beliefs and attitudes and our subconscious would have gone looking for evidence of something else instead, right? So let's give our subconscious some new evidence to get to work on proving instead.

Rather than believing those tired old stories anymore, I'd like to suggest another option: Substitute a newer, truer story in place of it. This transforms how we operate in the world, and what's most fascinating about that transformation is the impetus can be found in all the shit that used to drive us crazy when we were drinking. All the irritation we felt. All the problems we had. All the situations that seemed so unfair. All the people we thought should be different. All the blame we were portioning out to everybody around us.

You'll be happy to know that none of that was in vain. It's all grist for the mill, where the seeds of your transformation lie. This is the energy that's going to turn Drinking You into the Juicy AF You.

You'll also be happy to know that while Freud sees things as very fixed, there's new psychological research showing what has the biggest impact on our present situation is our vision of our future. Martin Seligman, the grandfather of positive psychology, collaborated on research that determined people who are trapped in the present or the past simply don't have a big enough concept of themselves in the future. Paint a picture of where you're going, why that matters to you, and then start acting like your awesome future self now.

You might be asking yourself: *But HOW do I change my tired stories into newer, more helpful ones?* By applying the antidote. Whatever the old story is, tell yourself the truth that lies opposite it.

| Old Story | I'm a victim. |
|---|---|
| Sounds Like | "He is such an asshole." |
| | "It's her fault that this happened to me." |
| | "I can't do X, because they won't let me." |
| New Operating System | I get to choose how to live. |

When you blame someone else for how and where you are in life, you are unnecessarily casting yourself as a victim. Once again, I am not victim-blaming here. The reality is, bad shit happens. I work with one woman who was kidnapped as an adult and another who was sex trafficked in her twenties. It shouldn't have happened, but it did.

Whatever your bad shit is, I want you to know you did not cause it—and now you have a choice. Do you really want your trauma to determine your health and well-being from here on out? Because that's what happens when you stay stuck in a victim mindset. I don't know about you, but I sure don't want whatever and whoever harmed me to control the rest of my life.

Your new operating system from here on out is *I get to choose how I live the rest of my life, how I think about it, how I perceive it, how I feel about it, and the actions I take.* You are in charge of your life, not whoever hurt you.

Take back your power.

| Old Story | I need to be different than who I am in order to be okay. |
|---|---|
| Sounds Like | "If I were more (something I'm not—fill in the blank), I would be happy." |
| New Operating System | The more vulnerable and truthful I am, the more people are attracted to me. |

It was extremely difficult for me to grow up in a family of quiet scientists where everything was beige. I was so clearly not that, it made me feel like how I was in the world was inherently wrong. As a result, I did a lot of pretending to fit in.

Like I said before, at one point in my life, I truly thought the reason people seemed happier than me was simply because they were pretending better. It never occurred to me that the answer was anything else. It made me even more insecure. I thought I wasn't even good enough at pretending!

Throughout it all, I was afraid to express who I really was. I believed if I revealed my true self, I would be cast out, ridiculed, banished, separated. Where I got that idea, who knows, but that was the story I made up to make sense out of my experience.

Especially when it comes to social media these days, it seems like everyone is wrapped up in presenting a façade that everything is great and perfect. We think we have to pretend to have it all together, all of the time. This is incredibly counterproductive and only makes us feel even less okay as we are.

The truth is people are absolutely gobsmacked by authenticity and vulnerability. That's what draws in love. What helps you truly connect with other people. What brings you closer together.

This is why it feels like such a giant relief when you meet someone who doesn't insist on pretending, speaks from the heart, and knows how to say things like "I don't know how to do this" or "I made a mistake, I was completely wrong, can you please forgive me?"

The antidote for feeling like you have to change in order to be accepted is knowing the more vulnerable and truthful you are, the more people are attracted to you. Vulnerability is how you win. It shows real strength.

Forget about putting on a dog and pony show for other people. Be you, authentically and openly.

| Old Story | I am unlovable as I am (aka I'm not good enough). |
|---|---|
| Sounds Like | "I need to do more, be more, and accomplish more." |
| New Operating System | I'm uniquely qualified to help. |

This one is pervasive and deep for a lot of us. We think our accomplishments equal our value and worth to this world, and without those we are unlovable. Maybe even nothing at all.

Part of this is due to the media. Part of it is our culture. Part of it is being a woman within a patriarchy that requires us to be conversant in male to succeed.

All I know for sure is that none of it ever felt genuine to me. I always felt like I was leaning a little off center. The story I created as a result was that I was somehow insufficient.

The antidote for this is knowing you are uniquely qualified to be helpful to a variety of people, in a variety of situations. Your experiences and talents ensure that you are needed in this world. I volunteer whenever the opportunity arises, and it never fails to help soothe any lingering doubts I may have about my contribution to the world.

This requires living in gratitude and service. If there are dishes to wash, push up your sleeves and dive in. If there are people who need help staying sober, be a kind and steady AF friend to them. If there are posters to be hung or meals to deliver, grab your tape or hop in the car. Don't wait to be asked; offer first. Your efforts will be widely appreciated.

Knowing you are here to help, and providing that assistance without being asked, is what it takes to realize you are lovable, worthy, and needed in this world. Don't deprive yourself or others of that gift. You are a joy to have here.

| Old Story | I'm an imposter. |
|---|---|
| Sounds Like | "If they only knew…"<br><br>"I can't ask for help because then they'll know I don't belong here." |
| New Operating System | Asking for help brings connection. |

I see this especially with younger women in business. They feel like, "If anyone knew the truth that I have no idea what the fuck I'm doing, I'd be fired/hated/banished immediately!"

But guess what? You're not supposed to know all the answers already. You get to ask for help. Doing so doesn't reveal anything bad about yourself or prove you have fatal shortcomings—it simply proves you're human like the rest of us.

Nobody is ever going to think less of you if you ask for clarification. Saying, "I don't have experience in this yet, can you help?" is not only your right, but also completely the right thing to do. No one knows everything. And we're all just making it up as we go.

Helping others is what gives our lives meaning. It's how we connect. That means acting like we're "bullet-proof" means we're making ourselves "connection-proof." For a long time, I thought if I impressed people, they'd like me, and I'd be okay. What I have experienced is the opposite. The more I matter-of-factly admit what I'm not good at, what I need help with, and where I need direction or reassurance, the more I connect with other people.

You already know plenty, just not the thing you are about to learn right now. Learning is growth. Keep moving forward.

| Old Story | I need you to change to make me comfortable. |
|---|---|
| Sounds Like | "Oh my God. I cannot believe she did that! She really should do something different. Blah, blah, blah..." |
| New Operating System | It's okay to be uncomfortable. |

The fact is, no one is going to change to make you more comfortable. The world is not designed for your comfort.

I recently read a really interesting book called *The Comfort Crisis* that argues that the comfort our society has brought most of us, most of the time, is actually deleterious to our mental, physical, and spiritual health. I mean, we have fucking heated steering wheels! I love them, and I can also see how they make us less resilient. A constant environment populated by things like that makes us feel like we can't handle anything anymore.

The new operating system here is, it's okay to be uncomfortable. It's not going to kill you and will more than likely teach you something. As basketball legend and coach Dawn Staley tells her players, "Growth takes place outside of your comfort zone."

Be brave enough to get uncomfortable and grow. The trick here is to get comfortable being uncomfortable. Discomfort isn't going to kill you. Your choice is to stay stagnant and comfortable, or to grow.

| Old Story | It's my job to ensure your happiness. |
|---|---|
| Sounds Like | "Are you okay? Do you want anything? Why don't I do X, Y, or Z for you?" |
| New Operating System | The only happiness I'm responsible for is my own. |

Women especially tend to do this with our kids and husbands. But the truth is, we cannot be responsible for someone else's happiness. If that is our goal, we will fail time and time again.

Rushing in to "protect" our loved ones' happiness only serves to send the message that we believe they are incapable of taking care of themselves. It's not saving the day. It's doing them a disservice.

Where do we get off thinking that we know what's better for anyone but ourselves anyway? The truth is, sometimes I don't know what's best for me, as evidenced by my choice of a first husband, my drinking, and my former motley assortment of dates. As my kids have gotten older, it's become very clear they've chosen their own paths. I can't give them advice for their lives, I can only give them advice for my life—and they don't want my life.

The way we learn is through experience, so don't try to save someone in the name of keeping them "happy." Every single person has a right to learn their own lessons in their own way. If we want people to extend that dignity to us, we owe them the same in return.

## Mind Your Own Mind

Now you've examined your old, tired beliefs and stories—the things that have been holding you back for so long—and are working to see yourself in a new light. You understand the power of your thoughts and mind. You know it's all in how you look at things.

The truth is, we all have the power of choice around our interpretation of anything. Think about Victor Frankl, author of *Man's Search for Meaning.* He was in two different concentration camps during World War II. His pregnant wife and his entire family were killed in the Holocaust. And yet he became one of the leading thinkers and teachers about finding meaning in life. That's how he chose to look at his circumstances.

We all have that same power. We can think about our experiences and say, "Damn, I learned a lot from that. Now I get to try something different." The magic happens when we do so consciously, taking responsibility for our part of creating where we are now, keeping whatever we're enjoying, and transforming the rest.

## BREAKOUT EXERCISE:
## MEDITATION TO RAISE YOUR VIBRATION

*Most of us get caught in our thoughts. We think just because we thought something, we have to take it seriously. Meditation offers the opportunity to observe our thoughts without attaching any meaning to them. It's like watching a river flow by rather than being carried away by it.*

*We choose all the time what thoughts we're going to engage in and which we're going to ignore, which sensations we're going to notice and which ones we're going to pretend don't exist. We do this unconsciously all day long—but yet another great thing about being sober is being able to play with this CONSCIOUSLY.*

*I believe spirit and awareness are linked. If I can notice my thoughts, feelings, and world from a place of neutral awareness, I am operating from spirit. Then I can consciously choose where I want to invest myself. Now I get to decide where I'm going to direct my attention and energy, and so do you.*

*Here's a great way to start meditating:*

- *Sit in a chair with your feet on the floor. Stack your shoulders over your hips and your ears over your shoulders.*
- *If it's comfortable, close your eyes. If it's not, cast your eyes downwards toward a spot about two feet in front of you.*
- *Take three deep, slow breaths. (This is your body's signal that you're going inward.)*
- *Simply count your exhales.*

- *Count up to ten.*
- *Start over at one.*

*Here's what is most likely to happen: Your mind is going to start screaming at you. You have too much to do to just sit here. Your nose itches (and now your nose is itching, and so is mine). Is that a kid calling you? What about that to-do list?*

*Perfectly expected. This does not make you "bad" at meditating. This makes you human.*

*Simply. Gently. (Gently, gently.) Return your attention to your exhales and start over at one.*

*When you notice you are at seventeen or you've mentally counted "six" endlessly, simply and gently (gently, gently) return your attention to your breath and start over at one.*

*Set your timer for thirty seconds.*

*Yep.*

*Thirty seconds.*

*It's far more important to develop a practice of doing this every day than to engage in a marathon meditation session once in a while.*

*If you make your starting goal laughably small, you won't get so flooded with fear that you don't start. It's a way of tiptoeing around that sleeping dragon of fear and engaging in this new behavior.*

*If thirty seconds starts feeling like not enough, set your timer for forty-five seconds or whatever feels comfortable to you.*

*I like to end a meditation session by establishing one thing I'm grateful for.*

*Then go about your day!*

*Meditation. Done and dusted.*

# CHAPTER SEVEN

# Spiritual Law #3

## GET OFF YOUR ASS AND DO SOMETHING

Your goal for this chapter: To move forward—even if you aren't "ready." Your feelings will soon catch up with your actions.

This chapter introduces the concepts of the Spiritual Principles (in essence, how to actually APPLY the Spiritual Laws in your life), changing your actions to change your thoughts, and practicing to perfect what you're learning here. It is designed to give you something to DO while waiting for the Spiritual Laws to take hold. Basically, it's about getting off your ass and making positive changes to your life starting now.

You don't change by hoping and wishing to change. You change by changing. You don't have to wait. You have to take action.

In "those meetings," they say, "If you want self-esteem, do estimable things," so we're going to focus on doing estimable things now. Yes, we are all human and will slip up in this endeavor, but we will also get it right many more times than that. Celebrate the estimable things you do, forgive yourself any missteps, and get right back on track.

If you want to create a story in your head that change is hard, miserable, painful, and takes a long time, that's your prerogative. Go ahead. But what I am offering you is a way to start acting like your ideal future self today, no slogging or misery necessary.

## Enacting Spiritual Principles in Your Life

So far, we've talked about Spiritual Laws. These explain how the spiritual dimension works, and they are your roadmap to a Juicy AF life. The more you act in accordance with them, the more spiritual power is going to flow through you.

Spiritual Principles, on the other hand, are the qualities and characteristics you want to imbue in your actions when practicing the Spiritual Laws. Think eulogy values here. These are how you ENACT the Spiritual Principles.

There are ten main Spiritual Principles: honesty, forgiveness, humility, acceptance, amusement, willingness, tolerance, gratitude, service, and patience. I invite you to investigate your relationship with each and delve further into how you can bring your actions into better alignment with them.

Spiritual Principles are powerful antidotes to the Old Stories we discussed in the previous chapter:

- Instead of pretending, I am honest.
- Instead of blaming, I forgive.
- When I feel arrogant, I remind myself to be humble.
- In place of taking myself seriously, I laugh at myself.
- When I stubbornly insist that I am right, I invite a smidgen of willingness.

114

- I substitute tolerance for being irritated at someone.
- When I'm focusing on getting more, I redirect to dwelling in gratitude for what I already have.
- When I feel anxious, insecure, and self-conscious, being of service brings relief.
- Oh, and since I am always in a fucking hurry, practicing patience is an ongoing, well, practice for me.

Substituting these Spiritual Principles for my old crazy-making attitudes and perceptions brings relief. It's not as fast as the relief I experienced from a sip of vodka, but it's more long-lasting and it brings long-term beautiful benefits.

Where to start? My suggestion is to begin by practicing one Spiritual Principle at a time. Bird by bird, as spiritual writer Anne Lamott says.

The way I integrate the Spiritual Principles into my own life is by focusing on one every week. I can remember to focus on honesty if it's the only Spiritual Principle I am thinking about. If I set myself up to practice all ten, chances are, I won't practice any.

My goal is to learn all I can about how each specific principle works or can work in my life. To begin, I brainstorm everything I think I know about that principle and write it down in my journal.

Next, I ask myself, what do I WANT to believe about this principle? What can I choose to believe that's going to give me inner peace? With those answers, I begin to experiment with believing those things for the next seven days.

Finally, I turn my attention to: How can I practice this Spiritual Principle at work? How can I apply it with my friends? My spouse? My children? Finding ways to incorporate the Spiritual Principle to enhance relationships always provides a positive experience for us all.

As I conduct these experiments, I'm always asking myself, what did I learn? What did I experience? And how am I going to apply that in my life going forward?

This becomes a very interesting way to live because every moment is an invitation to discover something new about myself and the world. If I'm only aspiring to be a better person, that isn't specific enough for me. Having one principle to have at the forefront of my mind for seven days in a row is what helps me achieve spiritual growth and spiritual traction.

In my experience, breaking down the Spiritual Principles into even smaller pieces helps deploy them more effectively. Each has similar component parts: a physical level, an intellectual level, and an emotional level. Addressing each of these can have a powerful transformative effect on how we practice the Spiritual Laws, and what information we receive in return.

Consider this your invitation to practice one Spiritual Principle this week. Here's how.

## COMPONENT #1: PHYSICAL

To begin, consider the physical component of the principle you're focusing on. The posture of pride is different from the posture of humility, right? The posture of lying is different from the posture of honesty. The posture of anger is different from the posture of forgiveness.

So if I'm focusing on being of service, what might that look like? It could be something in an outstretched hand. It's giving, not getting.

Or sometimes this exercise is easier to access from the opposite. In that case you can ask yourself, *okay, what's the opposite posture— selfishness? What does THAT look like?* Maybe that's someone holding onto something very tightly so no one else gets it.

The invitation here is to experiment with the physical manifestation of whatever Spiritual Principle you are working on, and then write about what you noticed. Whenever your brain thinks about it, check in to see how you're holding your body throughout the day. Is your posture more selfish or more of service? It's that simple.

The way we hold our bodies actually changes our emotions. It's been proven that smiling—even when you don't feel like it—tricks the brain into happiness. This stuff really matters, so concentrate on it.

## COMPONENT #2: INTELLECTUAL

Next, examine what you intellectually know about that Spiritual Principle. Let's use honesty as an example here. When I was a teenager, my mom would always ask who I was going out with, and I'd always say my girlfriends. My boyfriend would be there, too, but I didn't tell her about that part. That's a lie of omission. So now one thing we know is that honesty does not include lies of omission.

As you go through your day, now you can ask yourself, *am I telling everything that is pertinent about this situation? Am I holding something back? Am I lying by omission? What would it feel like if I told the complete truth?* Write about that experience. What did you notice? What did it feel like? Was it easier to tell the entire truth to a stranger than to your spouse, or just the opposite?

Another thing I think about: Through experimentation and practice, I've found that Spiritual Principles taken to the nth degree can be really dangerous and harmful. So then the question becomes, does that principle need to be tempered with something else? For example, to me, honesty without kindness is cruel. Honesty without appropriateness sets me up to be exploited. I look to find the best middle ground.

## COMPONENT #3: EMOTIONAL

Finally, examine the emotional piece of things and make note of your emotional reaction to whatever principle you're working on. Try to parse out what's driving your feelings and how to address them in a healthy way. How can you work through them?

For example, I learned karate as a grown-up. When I was a white belt, the sensei wanted me to learn a new skill from a green belt—

who happened to be a ten-year-old kid. I was thirty-five at the time, and it felt humiliating to still be at such a beginning stage of things. So I had to ask myself, *how can I do this but still have dignity?* And then I had to act accordingly.

To dig deeper into my emotions, I look at my resistance to the principle. For instance, to me acceptance connotes being passive and letting shit fly. How can I possibly reconcile genocide or kids being shot in a school? That's just not fucking acceptable. So then I ask myself how that unacceptable thing and my acceptance can live in the same place at the same time. Usually, the answer is that I need to take some action. I can't know that something is wrong and not DO something about it, so I take action.

It's important to realize here that any good thing taken to the extreme can become a bad thing. There needs to be the ballast over the bow of the ship. There's honesty, but that has to be tempered with kindness, wisdom, judgment, discernment, and diplomacy. There's kindness, but at some point, kindness ends and codependency starts.

Try to consider all these aspects as you apply the principles in your life. Going back to my days as a musician, a string vibrates because it's pinned down at the top and the bottom, and it's what's between those poles that makes the music. In the same way, we have to temper our actions. How can we be honest AND kind? What's the right vibration? Where's the point that feels right?

## Effort = Ego

Applying the Spiritual Laws to your life is being proactive in a different kind of way than you're probably used to, but there's nothing passive about it. This isn't about manifesting. It is, in fact, the exact opposite of magical thinking, and requires getting really clear about what you want, imbuing that with some feeling, and then RELAXING into it.

As someone with a super Type A personality, it felt so confounding when this concept was introduced to me. I wanted step-by-step instructions on how to relax. I felt like screaming, *But what exactly do I DO?*

My entire life, I have been career-first. I traveled, stayed late, and worked weekends. I only wished I would spin faster so I could achieve more. It felt like a counterweight to my narrative that I wasn't good enough. *Look, I'm a senior vice president—that must mean I'm worthy, right?*

Today, I actually get better results by relaxing. I have my best, most powerful ideas when I'm hiking. Whenever I get stuck, I put on my boots, go for a hike, and I come back in two and a half hours with the ideas I need.

What I've learned through experience is this: Where there's effort, there's ego. Not that having an ego is bad—we'd all starve and be unclothed without one. We have to learn to give it a rest sometimes so our spiritual energy can get to work for us. That energy is what will make us whole and happy. It is what takes care of the sense of shame, lack, and unworthiness that drove us to drink in the first place.

## Let It Be Easy

Can the Spiritual Principles of the universe transform the way you feel about yourself overnight? Absolutely! Why not? This is about shifting your consciousness and using all the buoyancy and energy you used to spend on just trying to keep your head above water so you can breathe on reimaging your life.

Getting where you want to go doesn't have to be a slog—it can be light and joyful and playful. I have chosen to believe that things are going to be easy, and so they are. I'm giving you permission to hold out the possibility that EVERYTHING in your new Juicy AF life can just be easy, effortless, and enjoyable too.

Remember, there's no "should" about any of this. This is merely an invitation to come to experiment. My mom lives in a retirement community and when I was visiting her the other day, she was talking about a woman that recently moved in. She said, "I really like her, but she walks ponderously. She's overweight. She is always down in the dumps. Her hair is mousey. I'm going to give her a red scarf." I told her, "Mom, you could experiment with simply accepting her for where she is and then deciding whether or not you want to spend time with her." And she was like, "Oh, right, I should do that."

As Denis Morton, my favorite Peloton instructor likes to say, "I make suggestions, you make decisions." I'm not dictating here. I don't think I have all the answers—just some ideas to help you draw insights and make conclusions about what makes you feel better and happier.

We're playing a game of hide and seek here, and I want you to join in. It's inclusive and invitational. Try working with one of these Spiritual Principles a week and see what happens.

## Start Taking Action!

I have a bias for action because I've learned the way I best incorporate changes into my life is by taking new actions. I've also learned that taking new actions often feels completely wrong at first. Don't worry. New actions eventually become ingrained and feel normal once you practice them enough.

For people with drinking problems whose baseline state is more anxious and agitated than perhaps it used to be, action is a great antidote. Action discharges that nervous energy into forward movement. It lessens the perseverating and buildup of pressure and anxiety.

## How Our Thoughts Drive Our Actions

Before we jump into our action-packed agenda any further, though, let's take a quick look at how what we think drives what we do, for better or for worse. I want to impart to you how strongly our perceptions impact our actions. Using my former drinking life as an example:

- I thought I drank because I had a crazy, chaotic, problem-filled existence. Of course, I needed to drink to take the edge off! The truth is, I had it backwards. I had a crazy, chaotic, problem-filled existence BECAUSE I drank. It goes back to that idea of homeostasis and how my biology had been forced to reset my baseline. Because drinking relaxes and calms the body, my body had to create the opposite—anxiety and irritability—so when I drank, I didn't get SO relaxed that my heart stopped beating. So in fact, it was the drinking that CAUSED the anxiety that provoked my chaos-filled decisions and actions, not my life's anxiety and chaos that caused the drinking.

- I thought my drinking was normal because I hung out with people who drank like I did. The truth is, my drinking was definitely abnormal compared to, say, the rest of the world's population. Once again, I had it backward. We see what we want to see. We look for proof that we are right, even when we are wrong. Now that I don't drink, I've noticed at weddings, for example, that there are maybe eight drunk people while everybody else has one glass of champagne and is done—not the other way around.

- I thought a life without alcohol would be infinitely worse than my drinking life. Truly, I thought people who didn't drink were hopelessly earnest do-gooders that hung out at the library on Friday nights. And I for sure did NOT want to be that person. The truth is, my drinking life was small, getting smaller, and ran on repeat. My AF life is expansive, adventurous, and fun, in all those amazing ways I listed earlier in this book.

- I thought I could solve my teeny, tiny drinking problem using the same self-will and discipline I used to solve my other problems, like leaving a bad marriage, working toward a promotion, or landing a new job. The truth is that I was addicted, and no amount of willpower was sufficient to solve my "little" issue.

How we perceive the world is what we experience. So when our perceptions are actually misperceptions—like mine were about my drinking—it inevitably leads to unwise actions. Life gets so much better when we uncover where those misperceptions are coming from and reframing them than continuing to believe them.

For example, what I found was that lurking underneath those misperceptions about my drinking was my perception of MYSELF and my place in the world. How I thought about myself was so painful it led me to loving the "comfortably numb" of drinking or being high. Although I couldn't see it at the time, my lack of self-love and compassion were really what drove me to drink.

My core belief about myself was that I was existentially not good enough. Not thin enough, pretty enough, rich enough, whatever enough. Or its corollary belief: I'm way too much. Too loud, over-dressed, too show-offy. And so everywhere I looked, I found more evidence of those core beliefs: I didn't get the promotion I wanted at work (not successful enough), the guy I thought I had rapport with at the party didn't call (not sexy enough), my kids' Halloween costumes came from Party City (not a good enough mom).

That's what always made the first drink sound like a good idea. Over time and with repeated drinking, my biology ensured that the first drink always happened. And my addiction (having no "off switch") always ensured I kept right on drinking.

That thought spiral had an incredibly strong gravitational pull. The only way to release myself from it was by THINKING differently and DOING differently. It was like playing "opposite day" every day.

Without making those changes, everything would have stayed the same, ad infinitum, and I am so grateful I chose to take a different path. It wasn't easy at first, but it was certainly easier in the long run than hating myself and my life and blowing up my relationships and career. What's more, it got easier and easier as I took one step forward and then another until I reached the beautiful life I'm living today.

## Change Your Actions to Change Your Mind

Basically what I'm saying here is, I thought myself into a drinking problem. Once I changed my actions, that changed my thinking. And once my thinking and perceptions changed, those new actions began to seem normal and automatic.

My thoughts led to actions that kept me in the spiral. Changing my thoughts—and as a result, my actions—are what got me out of it. Now it's your turn to do the same.

How? By using the same power of thought that's keeping you in the spiral to remove yourself from it. Our inner dialogue is our kingdom. We have complete control and complete responsibility for what goes on in there. That is our God-given, divine spirit and innate power.

You might be protesting, "But I was abused as a child or endured some other type of hideous trauma—THAT'S why I drink!" While I hear you, I'm also not going to coddle you. I love and respect you too much to not be direct with you.

You are a grown woman. You are NOT a victim. You get to choose how you perceive any situation.

Once again, I am not victim-blaming here. Whatever happened to you should NEVER have happened. But the fact is, it did. So now the question becomes, what are you going to do about it? Are you going to let that crappy person or environment or tragedy have dominion over the rest of your life? Does it get to be bigger than you, and you must remain smaller and powerless to change how your life plays out from there? My answer to that is a resounding no. Absolutely not.

Second, you don't get to be here on earth without enduring some difficult things. That's called life. But while we may not get to choose our trials, we damn well do get to pick how we move forward from them. So pick something better than where you are at the moment. Pick yourself. Champion a new you.

Decide you're willing to endure some short-term pain for lasting, loving, life-affirming, long-term gains. This is no small feat, but it is also infinitely doable. I'm here to guide, provoke, and challenge you to let go of your old stories and create your new juicy AF operating system. Have a little faith, experiment, and play.

Think of it this way: You're already here reading a quit-lit book. You know what that tells me? You're in enough pain to try something different. So starting now, I challenge you to take responsibility for the thoughts you entertain, the perceptions and stories you create, and the actions you choose. You might wish there was another path to health and happiness, but there is not.

## Actions First, Feelings Follow

The first steps we take toward a new way of thinking and being happen in the context of our old lives. By default, that means it's going to feel weird at first. It's going to go against every instinct you have. And that's okay.

Just know all this is coming. There's nothing wrong with you. There's nothing wrong with what you're doing. Your body and brain are just having a moment, realizing things are changing, and then figuring out how to adjust to those changes. They are searching for ways to find a new homeostasis.

That feels very weird. It feels very vulnerable. Do it anyway.

I used to think I had to be in the right mind space to change. That I had to be feeling it before I took action. The newsflash to me was that it's actually easier to change your mind by changing your actions than to change your thinking first. Take the actions first and your feelings will follow.

This requires a smidgen of willingness to experience the discomfort of doing something that you KNOW is bullshit and won't work. I find it easier to take a new action when I hold it as an experiment for a finite amount of time. Why not meditate for two minutes every day for fourteen days and then evaluate what's working and what's not working?

## Practice Perfects

I started playing cello when I was eight. I majored in cello at Northwestern University (a very useful degree, I'm sure you'll agree). I played in the civic orchestra in Chicago (a semi-professional affiliate of the Chicago Symphony). That's how I became an expert in practicing.

When you play the cello, there are notes, there's rhythm, there's bowing, and there's intonation. I had to consider all these elements when playing a musical passage. And for far too long, my practice method consisted of playing the same passage at the same speed in the same way.

Somehow, I'd always fuck up in the same place, so I'd have to start over from the beginning. I'd play, fuck up, start over. Play, fuck up, start over. Play, fuck up again, start over. I went in that infuriating circle for years (kinda like my drinking spiral).

What I finally discovered—probably too late to do me much good—was if I slowed things way down, broke up the musical passage into its component parts, and practiced each one separately, only then could I start to put things back together correctly. Now THAT'S an effective way to practice.

Learning to do something well—like how not to drink—can only come through practice, just like I practiced playing the cello. I know we've all been taught practice makes perfect (and boy, did we per-fect those old crappy stories) but we're not aiming for perfection here. Instead, we're aiming to simply create new healthy habits in our lives.

We're always practicing something. The difference this time is you are CHOOSING what you practice.

---

## BREAKOUT EXERCISE:
## ENERGY WORK

*I believe we're all spirits living in human bodies. A beam of light runs down our central column—which is where our spirit lives—providing power to our seven energy centers that live along it. The first energy center is located at the base of the spine, the second is two inches below the navel, and the third one is right below the ribs. The fourth is in the center of the chest, the fifth in the throat, the sixth behind the eyes, and the seventh in the center of the head. (Some people refer to these as chakras.)*

*When our bodies are tense and exerting maximum effort, that spiritual channel gets constricted. The more effort we put out, the tighter the aperture. Once the body relaxes, that spiritual channel begins to reopen.*

*Try to imagine now what the beam of light powering YOUR energy center looks like. What color is it? Silvery sparkly pink? Glittery blue and gold? Majestic matte purple?*

*What does it feel like? Effervescence? Silk? Fuzzy pajamas?*

*Experiment with widening and narrowing your beam of light. Become aware of it. Play with it. Work with it.*

*It's crazy how things flow to me and through me when that inner channel of light is wider, bigger, more robust. I don't have to work so hard. Have faith that it's going to come to you like that, too.*

*Being in a relaxed place tells the universe I have faith— in both it and myself. That you're willing to work WITH it instead of against it. That you're ready to go frolic in the spiritual playground.*

---

# CHAPTER EIGHT

# Spiritual Law #4

## FORGIVE TO GET FREE

**Your goal for this chapter: Forgive who and whatever you are angry with or hurt by and free yourself from them.**

According to my mom, I was a "handful." So much so, apparently, that she had to go take a course based on the book *I'm Okay, You're Okay* to learn how to navigate her relationship with me. (She has told me in retrospect that she realizes she was also very reactive to her mom when she was a teen. Oh, hi there, karma.)

At one class, my mom was upset with my grandma. The leader assumed the role of my grandma, took one end of a scarf in her hand, and asked my mom to grab onto the other end. The teacher then started yanking the scarf all over the place. As my mom describes it, she was holding on for dear life and being whipped around by what her "mom" was doing and saying. The teacher then said to my mom, "Let go of your end of the scarf," and of course, the whiplash immediately stopped.

That was such a revelation to her. All she had to do was stop engaging in the battle. She just had to let go of her end of that damn scarf.

When we haven't forgiven someone, it's the same thing as my mom still holding onto to the end of that scarf. We're letting them whip us around, whip up all this anger, keep the hurt alive. But guess what? We can also choose to let it go.

We can choose to be FREE.

## Getting Untangled

The translation of the Lord's Prayer most of us know comes from the King James Bible—*forgive us our sins, as we forgive those who sin against us*—but there's this amazing translation of it from the Aramaic that's just unbelievable. It says:

> Oh, cosmic Birther of all radiance and vibration, soften the ground of our being and carve out a space within us where your Presence can abide.
>
> Fill us with Your creativity so that we may be empowered to bear the fruit of Your mission. Let each of our actions bear fruit in accordance with our truest desire that You set in our hearts.
>
> Endow us with the wisdom to produce and share what each being needs to grow and flourish.
>
> **Untie the tangled threads of destiny that bind us, as we release others from the entanglement of past mistakes.**
>
> Do not let us be seduced by that which would divert us from our true purpose but illuminate the opportunities of the present moment.

For You are the ground and the fruitful vision, the birth,
power, and fulfillment, as all is gathered and made whole
once again.

I absolutely love the whole thing, especially the line that says
*Untie the tangled threads of destiny that bind us, as we release others
from the entanglements of past mistakes.* The way I read this is we get
entangled with other people when they piss us off. They hurt us, and
those hurts are the past mistakes the end of the line is referring to.

Now think about that. Do you really want to be entangled with
somebody you have a beef with forever? Of course not! I want to be
done with my ex-husband, I don't want to be entangled with him.

Want to know something else about these entanglements? Being
entangled with someone through anger or any other emotion means
you're ceding the authority of your inner state over to them. And
do you want to give them that dominion over your consciousness?
Hell, no!

I think people get hung up with forgiveness because they think
it means condoning whatever happened. That can look as large as
*if I forgive that person for being racist that will mean I'm condoning
racism*, or as small as *if I forgive someone that will mean I now want
to be friends again and invite them over for dinner.* We get all twisted
up in these intellectual debates when forgiving truly doesn't equal
condoning.

## But What if They're Complete Assholes?

Nobody wakes up in the morning and says, "I wonder how big of
an asshole I can be today?" We're all hypocritical at some point or
another. We say one thing and we do something else. We make decisions that are incomprehensible to others but obviously right to us.

When I was a market researcher most of my clients worked in
packaged foods, so I used to go grocery shopping with people to

gather information. On one of these trips, my shopper had a choice between buying regular potatoes and potatoes wrapped in foil with a sticker on them that said, "great for grilling." She grabbed a bunch of foil-wrapped ones even though they were three times the price of the regular ones. When I asked her to help me understand why, she said it was because she wanted to grill the potatoes. That made perfect sense to her—even though she also could have gone home and wrapped the regular potatoes in foil she already owned for way cheaper.

The point being, the way people go through life barging and shoving makes total sense to them, even when it is incomprehensible to us. They're not TRYING to be assholes. Besides, what we do is probably incomprehensible to them, too.

People need dignity, respect, and grace. They need open-mindedness. In their minds, what they're doing is totally justifiable. I used to look at people and think *What in God's name are they doing?* Now I just think *Well, that's their experience. They have to learn whatever they're going to learn in the way they're meant to learn it.* Every single one of us has a right to learn through experience. We've all got our own spiritual lessons to learn in this lifetime.

The next time someone is doing something incomprehensible to you, try to get curious about how that might make sense to the person doing it. Rather than labeling them as an asshole, ask yourself: Where is that true for me? Can I be okay with the humanity of that instinct? And if someone had treated me the way they were treated, how would I feel and act?

This exercise is really about trying to put yourself in somebody else's shoes. It's about recognizing that you have probably already been there, too. Maybe in a different way—maybe less violent or dressed up nicer—but still there.

For example, in my first marriage it seemed like all we did all day was try to convince the other person that we were right. If I said, "This shirt is blue," he'd argue that no, it was green. There was this ongoing struggle to win at all costs. This did not make for a happy marriage, by the way.

In "those" meetings, they say, "Do you want to be right or do you want to be happy?" (When I asked my daughter this question, she said both.) But all of the above is not one of the choices here. With my current husband, there is none of this kind of "who's right-er" kind of competition. Recently, we were watching somebody swim and he said, "Look, they're doing the crawl." In my head, I was like, *they're doing the breaststroke* but I didn't say a goddamn thing because who cares? Once they started swimming toward the shore, he revised his former position. "Oh, they're doing the breaststroke." We both ended up in the same place without any bickering or judgment, and we laughed about it.

I used to go to this therapist I call Saint Joan. She asked me one day, "How did you learn your biggest lessons?" My answer was by making big, painful mistakes. Her next question was, "Why would you deprive your children of that same opportunity to learn?" As a parent, I just found that concept so freaking hard. I seemingly did not get the memo that said when kids reach a certain age it is no longer appropriate for me to protect them—it's time for them to learn shit on their own.

One of my children was very distracted, disorganized during that really important junior and senior year when colleges are really looking at your grades. This kid would lose a piece of paper between the drop-off and walking in the door. I used to have a weekly call with his homeroom teacher, who would make sure that all of his homework was done. My son was eighteen at the time, and we were still checking in on him like he was in kindergarten!

In retrospect, would it have been better for him to fail then? Would it be better for him as an adult? Nothing I can do about it now, but probably yes (at the very least, I would feel better about my parenting).

So consider the fact that maybe the asshole isn't actually intending to be an asshole. Consider where they may be coming from and why. And then let them go learn their lessons their own way, in their own time.

## Going Deeper

As I said earlier, our anger is usually a mask for something else. It's misplaced. Even if something made you justifiably angry—anyone that happened to would get angry about it, too—it's never ONLY about that thing. There's always a secondary emotion hiding underneath there. Usually that's hurt or pain or loss. Dig deep using the breakout exercise at the end of Chapter Two: Triggers and How to Deal with Them to find out what that is.

Let's say you're caught in traffic and it's making you fume. Underneath all of that is feeling bad about not having left on time, right? You're mad at yourself, not the other cars around you. It's misplaced anger, because in some way you were complicit in creating the circumstance. You ignored red flags.

Again, I'm not trying to blame the victim here. Really, I'm not. If you were abused or raped or kidnapped, that's clearly not your fault. No one should be treated that way. But the question then becomes, how are you going to carry that experience going forward? Because what you ARE responsible for is your reaction to whatever happened.

For example, my youngest daughter was born into a really tough situation. Before we adopted her, she lived in an orphanage where she had limited interaction and physical contact for the entire first year of her life. The question for her now is, what do you want to do about it? That's her choice.

Have you ever gone scuba diving? When you jump off the boat, there's an anchor line, and the way you descend to where the coral and the parrotfish and the shrimp and all the cool stuff is is by pulling yourself down the rope. That's what I'm encouraging you to do here. Instead of staying where you are, looking at the whitecaps on the top of the water—the anger, the justification, the misery—I want you to keep going down that rope until you get to what's REALLY going on underneath all that anger.

And then I want you to forgive. Yourself for being human, and the other person for whatever they did.

## Find Your Freedom

I said to my mom once, "You keep describing me as having been a handful, but what do you mean by that? I wasn't sneaking out at night. I got excellent grades." She thought about that a bit and then told me, "I guess we just didn't understand anything about what you were interested in."

I already instinctively knew that. That's why the story that I came up with as a very young girl was *there is something wrong with me. I have to pretend to be something I'm not in order to be okay because I'm so different from my family. I need to find a way to fit in even if that means changing who I am.*

I used to say that the Queen of England had given birth to me. (I'm not grandiose or anything!) I decided she had dropped me off in this suburban house for my parents to raise me. I felt so different and weird and awkward, that's how I made sense out of my situation. We create stories all the time.

Once you can see old stories for what they are—which is, stories invented to make sense out of your experience—then the corollary is, now I can invent a new story. This is where the juice lies. This is what unlocks creating your future. This is our God-given, divine power.

So what do you want to live from moving forward? My guess is not anger, but forgiveness. And out of that comes freedom and joy.

Forgiveness gets rid of obstructions and occlusions and all the fuzzy, furry, gross shit growing in the corner of your refrigerator.

It clears your intuitive channel. And when we tap into that, we get back in touch with our knowingness and spirit.

I feel like we're told in Christianity that the reason we should be good and forgive is so that we're good enough for God. But forgiveness isn't something we "should" do to be good enough to deserve to find God. We are ALREADY part of God. Forgiveness just clears away what blocks God from being fully present in us.

So yes, forgiveness is freedom—both freedom FROM and freedom TO. Remember where we started with untying the tangled threads of destiny that bind us to the person we're pissed at? Forgiveness unties those threads. It frees you from somebody else jerking you around at the end of the scarf.

Once you're free from that, all of a sudden it makes you free to be more of a spiritual channel. To be more neutral. To choose your experiences consciously rather than staying where you've always been. Now that's JUICY.

In life, we really do get to choose our attitude. Are we going to be thrown into anger or hurt? Absolutely. I know I do. Welcome to being human. Upon reflection, though, we also get to choose whether we stay in that anger and hurt or focus on how much we love our Juicy AF life.

Choose freedom.

---

## BREAKOUT EXERCISE:
## FORGIVE THOSE FUCKERS

*One of the tools I learned in sobriety is to send blessings to the person I'm upset with every day. The instructions say to try it for two weeks. I think it took me two years with a certain person I used to be married to.*

*As I sent him daily wishes for prosperity and health and*

*wellbeing and happiness, I eventually realized that the happier and more whole he was as a person, the less of a jerk he was going to be. I also realized it would be better for my kids if he was whole and happy and prosperous. And that meant it would ultimately be better for me.*

*There isn't a limited supply of wholeness and happiness. If the person I'm pissed at gets to be happy in their own skin, it doesn't mean that I don't. It's not taking anything away from me.*

*That exercise really helped me lose my animosity and get to a place of being neutral. And that's the goal here—just to get to neutral, neutral, neutral. You don't have to love that person. You can be neutral about them.*

*So pray for the person you're so pissed at and wish them blessings. At the same time, wish yourself neutrality. Envision a giant neon sign over your head, that blinks* neutrality, neutrality. *Let that neutrality flood your system. Every time you think of that person, say to yourself, I'm neutral. Every time you're going to see that person, practice being neutral. Neutrality is where we want to get here. There's nothing another person can do to add or take away from the essence of who you are.*

*Remember how we talked about practicing in a previous chapter? This is a practice, too. Every time your mind starts thinking about the shitty things that person has done to you, redirect that into wishing them peace and prosperity and happiness and being comfortable in their own skin. The more you replace that pain and anger and loathing with the thought of blessing, the more it begins to sink in. Eventually, that will bring you to a place of neutrality. Your mind will start to believe you.*

*It's a matter of choosing your thoughts rather than letting* your thoughts run away with you like a wild horse down the beach dragging you by a stirrup. Be my mom on the end of that scarf. Let it go.

So pray for the motherfucker for thirty days. It's free. Try it. If you're still miserable and angry after a month, then move on to something else.

---

# CHAPTER NINE

---

# Spiritual Law #5

## CONNECTIONS ARE KEY

Your goal for this chapter: Find community and look for ways to be of service to others. Being connected is what serves you and others best.

One of the hallmarks of someone that drinks too much is that we think about ourselves a lot. We usually have social anxiety and can feel pretty self-conscious. Like, *what is everybody else thinking about me? What that person did was meant to hurt me.* It's this very solid, systematic way of seeing the world where everything in it is about us.

When it's all about us, that self-critical internal voice becomes all-consuming. All of our focus is on ourselves. *Oh, I have a little twinge of self-doubt. I better go think about that a lot. Where did that come from?* And *what's wrong with me* and *where was it in my past* and blah, blah, blah. The more we indulge in that, the less present we are in the world.

When we're in the center of our universe, everyone else is just a planet orbiting us. We're not in a relationship with anybody else. We're having a mediocre life devoid of good connections because we're holding people away from us.

If we turn around and always put another person in the center of our universe, then we start orbiting around THEM. That's called codependency. It's not much better than being focused only on ourselves.

But if we give other people as much weight as we give ourselves, then we're in the dance.

## Making the Copernican Shift

Remember Copernicus? He discovered that the sun doesn't revolve around the earth, the earth revolves around the sun. What we need to do here is make a Copernican shift from ME as the center of my universe to something bigger than me, or different than me, or at least something equal to me in the center of my universe.

What I've found is putting someone ELSE in the center for an appropriate amount of time means I don't have to be the center anymore. When we think about other people, it actually helps us realize we're grateful. We realize our lives are not so terrible after all.

For me, this book is my way of being of service to other women that are in the place I was twenty-something years ago. That gives my life so much meaning, but it also takes away some of my self-centeredness. It's not all about me now, it's about you, too.

Another example: I flew back to Chicago to support a friend whose husband was playing a piece that had been commissioned by the Chicago Symphony before he retired. He had just joined the symphony when we met, and this was the capstone. My friend and I were inseparable when our oldest kids were babies, so it was really important to me to show up for her.

So I attended the performance and then went to the party at

their house afterwards. I didn't know anyone there, so I actually ended up behind the bar pouring drinks for people. I was there for a purpose. Yes, I was there to support my friends and show up. But it wasn't about me at all, and I could see that there was a need, so I stepped in and took care of it. (And just so you know: I was touching bottles of booze all night and did not have one single iota of a craving to drink. This is what your life can become and what you have to look forward to, I promise.)

The Copernican shift also works really well when you put nature in the center rather than ME. If I can just be in nature in some way, it takes me out of myself. Out my window there is a bluebird mountain sky. There are pine trees with puddles of snow hanging from the branches. When the wind blows, the snow gets flung up into the air and it's just freaking extraordinary.

My recommendation is to go out into nature and get curious. Go for a walk in a park. Look at the texture of the bark or the way the light plays on the leaf of a tree. It doesn't take any money or any special equipment.

Put spiritual exploration at the center of your universe, too. Meditation works especially well to take me out of myself. Please consider meditation and God to be the same thing. A way to rest in the Divine.

## Aligning Yourself with the World's Deep Hunger

*The place God calls you to is the place where your deep gladness and the world's deep hunger meet.*

—Frederick Buechner

Being of service is another way to get out of our own heads, like I did when I became the stand-in bartender at the party celebrating my friend's husband. Try to contribute in a way where your greatest gift meets the world's deepest hunger. Maybe that's volunteering for a political campaign, cuddling senior dogs at the shelter once a week, or organizing a meal train for the family of a sick child.

Where we get lit up, what part of the world's deepest hunger we have experience with, and how we are uniquely suited and qualified to be healing and helpful is the place we need to be. That's where life and love happen. That's the connection. That to me is where the presence of God—you can substitute the word Love or Nature or the Universe here if you want—lives.

Imagine a net spun from pure gold, and inside the net are all these beautiful jewels. They sparkle and dance together, constantly radiating their gorgeous colors to the rest of the bunch. Well, that's us! When we are in our greatest gifts, we are those shining jewels, held together by the golden threads of loving relationships.

## Staying Connected

You may find your relationships shifting now that you're on this new path. Many people in your life will love the changes you've made and the woman you've become. Your connection with them will grow and expand in ways you might not have even imagined possible. That's the power of authenticity, vulnerability, and clarity in your life.

Others might not understand or approve of the "new you." In these cases, I've had to remember this is much likely more about them than it is you. Your growth is making that person recognize where they need to change, and they are not ready to do it. Support them with loving wishes but don't let them change your course.

Everyone is on their own path and at a different place of spiritual development. We all came into this life to learn, and those lessons will be taught in due time. It's not up to us how or when that happens.

So work to deepen your relationships with people you already know and love. Forgive those who don't vibe with where you are yet, and don't give up on them—they may just surprise you in the future. Be open to meeting new friends and exploring new experiences with them. Everyone we come in contact with has something to teach us and can help us grow.

Most of all, though, share your life with others. We are all here to support one another. As St. Augustine wrote, "Since you cannot do good to all, you are to pay special attention to those who, by the accidents of time, or place, or circumstances, are brought into closer connection with you." Spread your love, live your truth, share your gifts.

---

## BREAKOUT EXERCISE:
## USE YOUR SENSES

*Being in nature can be completely transcendent. It has the ability to take us out of any self-centered fear, anxiety, and preoccupation we might be feeling. See if you can be in it without putting labels on the experience (because as soon as you put a label on a tree or sunlight, it has the effect of flattening it out and somehow making it smaller and less beautiful).*

*Can you find a way to simply breathe and notice the details without thinking? Concentrate on your senses. What does it smell like? What does it look like? What's the quality of the light, the texture of the bark, or the softness of the rain? Take your shoes off. Feel the earth beneath your feet. Get grounded.*

*There, don't you feel better now?*

---

# CONCLUSION

I'VE ALWAYS BEEN an extremely disciplined person. When I was still drinking, though, I would start a thousand things and never finish any of them. (Imagine living in a household with that many unfinished projects—UGH!). I had such good intentions, but that's what the road to hell is paved with (according to my dad). What I'm getting at here is that everything you've learned in this book is great, but if you don't follow through and apply it to your life, your life will not change.

If you haven't already, start now. If you're already committed, be vigilant. Maintain alert awareness. Keep coming back to the Spiritual Principles. Stay strong. Do not waver—do something joyfully Juicy AF instead.

What we choose to think about gets bigger, right? What we focus on grows. So I want you to take personal responsibility for the vibe you send out in the world and the actions you take.

## Practice, Not Perfection

Vigilance is something you have to keep on practicing. Again, the aim is not perfection here. It's simply a continuation.

One of the other things I know from having been a professional musician is that part of practice is falling off. It's forgetting to do it. It's being too tired. It's being frustrated or being simply too bored to do it today. You just have to push on through that. Don't pick up a drink when you feel this way—fall back on one of your substitutions instead. You're prepared for it.

It's the same as meditation: Whenever you feel your brain galloping off with random thoughts, gently, gently, gently, bring your attention back to your breath. It's the gentle redirection that we all need to practice here. That's the key to doing anything new and sticking with it.

If you find yourself feeling like *here I am, in fear again and freaking out,* say to yourself, *I'm going to choose to take a deep breath, I'm going to choose to face that fear, and I'm going to choose to persist in finding the joy in life.* That's all it takes to keep going.

There are days I don't want to work out. I am just not feeling it. I don't want to do it. But in gentleness, I bring myself back and get it done anyway.

All that being said, don't let your expectations of yourself become too harsh or too punitive or too demanding. Be gentle and forgiving and loving with yourself. If you were trying to tame a wild horse, you wouldn't punish it for doing something wild. You'd talk to it slowly. Reassuringly. In what my son likes to call my "late night DJ voice." Very calm. Very slow. In a low register.

Remember: The only thing you have to do is KEEP GOING.

## Play!

Once you stop drinking, your life becomes an experimental playground. This is the joy you get to experience now that the shame spiral is over. This is what's going to bring out your sparkle.

I want you to think of all the things we've been talking about like a kindergarten dress-up box. Dig in and start experimenting. Put on the sorcerer's hat today and be a sorcerer. Even though this is essential to building a Juicy AF life, we don't have to be so serious about it. So bring the joy in. Make it fun. Bring that awesome vibe to it!

We can do important things in a light way. As soon as anything becomes ponderous, or heavy, or burdensome, the creative door to your imagination and curiosity slams shut and locks. So if you have an experience you like, do it again. If an exercise doesn't work for you, adjust it so it's a better fit or don't do it anymore. Simple as that.

Don't think, *oh, I'm a terrible person. I used to drink too much and now everything will be boring and shitty for the rest of my life.* Instead of beating yourself up with remorse and shame, adopt a mindset of *Cool, I get to finger paint today!* This attitude shift is what's going to heal you from the things that drove you to drink.

## Create a Joy-Filled Life

Johann Hari, a well-known journalist and author, did a TED Talk called "Everything You Know about Addiction is Wrong." In it, he discusses two experiments. In the first, researchers put a rat alone in a cage that contained two water bottles—one with plain water and one with heroin-laced water in it. That rat promptly overdosed and died from drinking the heroin water. So that must mean rats prefer heroin to water, right? Well, maybe not.

Eventually, another researcher came along and challenged that conclusion. They put a bunch of rats into a stimulating environment—there were wheels to run on and other rats to have sex with and tunnels to explore and places to burrow—along with the two water bottles. Those rats maybe tried the heroin water once, but they never went back to it. There was too much else to do and experience.

Johann's interpretation was that connection was what was missing from the first rat's environment, and that's what made it choose the heroin water. I'd argue that it was also a stimulating, joy-filled, interesting life that contributed to the rats in the second experiment not needing to numb out to get by.

And that's exactly what I'm inviting you to create for yourself—an exciting, stimulating, full inner world and outer world. A world that has enough of a mix of structure and stimulation that makes for an engaging, interesting existence. That takes trial and error.

Just as once a baby's nap rhythm stabilizes it changes again, the same thing happens to us as adults. The inner and outer environment that I have created now is such a better alternative to my drinking life—but where I was at two years sober is really different from where I am now twenty-something years sober. And it will be different again when I'm thirty years AF.

In other words, this is not a one and done kind of thing. As soon as you feel cranky and bored with what you've created, go back and create something new. Once you learn how to envision your future and create these experiences, you get to keep it going. It's a muscle that you learn to flex.

## Show Up, Shine Bright, & Live Juicy AF

So what's next? Well, now you:

- Accept the fact that drinking even a little isn't going to work for you. That might not feel like great news, but it's actually awesome news because what lies on the other side of putting down the bottle is an incredible life.
- Stop drinking if you haven't already and try a little willingness to be open to the idea that a life without drinking is possible.
- Apply the tools you learned in this book. Reading it once is fantastic. It's a huge step. But actually putting it into effect in your life is what's going to change your life.

- Feel how attractive a Juicy AF life can be—light-hearted, amusing, uplifting.
- Join the Juicy AF community so you can do all this learning and growing with other people who are focused on the same goals.

Our families, our community, and our world all need us to show up as the authentic, kind, hopeful, bright, Juicy AF women we are. We may get sober for ourselves, but I found—and I'm sure you will too—that our light brings joy, peace, and wisdom to everyone around us. I am inviting you to a Juicy AF life and showing you how to get there.

The rest? Well, that's up to you. I'll be here cheering you on the whole time, and so will all the Juicy AF women out there who are on the same journey.

Go forth and be joyful. Make your life the one of your dreams. And may you stay forever juicy, my friends.

# ACKNOWLEDGMENTS

---

It takes a village to create a book.

First, my thanks to the talented, funny, and spiritually-attuned Trish Cook, without whom I would have given up while outlining Chapter Five.

I've been blessed to work with a rock star team at Scribe Media: Eliece, Jess, Jennifer, and their compatriots.

And I am supported and challenged by my Juicy AF team: Renee, Tara, Thea, Sean, and Emily. And my team at NGNG Enterprises: Amber, Megan, Alexis, and your entire crew. You truly are amazing, resourceful, and ridiculously detailed.

I'm grateful beyond words to The Mountain Evening Meeting. I love, respect, and am inspired by each of you.

A bow of thanks to my first Juicy AF (aka KA) group: Colleen, Candice, Lynn, Marcia, Beth, Melissa, Annalise, Susan, Kris, Karen, and those that visited.

I'm grateful to Mary Bell Nyman and Lauren Skye for their training in the world of clairvoyance.

Marcia, thank you for being my first reader and my closest friend.

My life is brighter because of my children. I absolutely adore my kids: Claire, Anya, Christian, and Samantha. And a thank you to my husband John Donicht who makes me feel like I belong, who makes me laugh, and with whom I love to dance.

Made in the USA
Las Vegas, NV
10 January 2023